THE VIRTUOUS WOMAN

Proverbs 31:10
"Who can find a virtuous woman? For her price is far more precious than rubies."

"Virtuous woman, you are precious!
Through the Blood of Jesus."

P – *URE*

R – *ESPECT*

E – *NDURANCE*

C – *HASTE/COMMITTED*

I – *NTERCESSOR*

O – *BEDIENT*

U – *NDERSTANDING*

S – *ANCTIFIED*

Dr. Kate Love Lutterodt

by Drs. Richard G. and Phyllis J. Arno; authors of Creation
Therapy and founders of The Sarasota Academy of Christian
Counseling, Sarasota in Florida.

What Does the Bible Say About Women Ministers?
by Dr. William Michael Comfort B.A M.A.M. Litt. D. Phil,
N.D.F.I.B.A.
Chesapeake Bible College and Seminary, Maryland.

Cover picture designed by Marie – Claire Daou Revised
Edition 2007

www.xulonpress.com

DEDICATION
TO GOD ALMIGHTY,
ALL WOMEN
&

My children: Eva Bedford-Oppong, Ebenezer Adinkrah, Victoria Adinkrah, Emmanuel Adinkrah and Edward Adinkrah.

ACKNOWLEDGEMENT

A cknowledgement to God the Father, Son and Holy Spirit for abundant grace, love and sweet fellowship that has made this project a reality. My spiritual fathers, mentors, fellow ministers of the Gospel both in Ghana and the USA; space would not permit me to mention all your names. The good Lord knows you and will richly bless you; I cannot thank you enough; most especially ministers of God who took time to write forwards and endorsements for this book, and those who helped with the editing and type setting.

May God richly bless you all.

TABLE OF CONTENTS

FORWARDS

FORWARD I

Dr. Kate Love Lutterodt, an ordained minister of the gospel has provided the Christian community with an in-depth analysis of what it means to be a virtuous woman. Based upon her study and understanding of the biblical text in *Proverbs 31:10-31*, she analyzes the text through eleven carefully structured chapters. These chapters deal with the mystery of womanhood, creation of woman, the role of women ministry, marital relationships, soul-ties, how to destroy Satan's strongholds in our lives and creation therapy. The core of her analyses is in chapters three and five; in chapter three, Dr. Lutterodt examines the *"characteristics of Eve seen in women."*

Dr. Lutterodt boldly maintains that *"disobedience* and *disrespect"* are characters very typical of women." Here, she courageously gave the culture of *"me-first"* and situational ethics rampant in our modern society. In America and virtually most parts of the world respect has been thrown out of marital relationships! But Dr. Lutterodt also outlines what are the *"biblical rights of women"* which offers a balance to her study.

In chapter five, Dr. Lutterodt offers the steps to becoming a virtuous woman and summarizes such qualities. There is much sensible and practical advice in her book for today's mother and wife, especially a Christian woman. There are also many spiritual citations to support her position. Indeed, husbands ought to read this book for information as it reveals a woman's perspective on marital relationships.

I commend Dr. Lutterodt for her efforts in literature, evangelism and ministry to women and strongly recommend her book to the reading public.

E.S. Etuk, Ph. D.
Award –winning Author of 8 Books, & President
Emida International Publishers
www.emidal.com
www. Authorsandexperts.com

FORWARD II

In the "*Virtuous Woman*" Dr. Lutterodt presents one of the varied approaches to the way the *Proverbs 31* woman could be viewed. In this one person resides all the desirable characteristics and qualities of a woman, a wife, a mother and a god-fearing person. Those who seriously read this book will be blessed.

Rev. Dr. Stephen K. Gyermeh
Senior Pastor & Founder
The Church of the Living God
Full Gospel Ministries, Inc.
Maryland U. S. A.

FORWARD III

I have always believed that when preparation meets opportunity, success will explode; in other words, success becomes the end result. Many, especially *"Women"* who aspire to succeed in their marriage unions, in the corporate world and in their social relationships just assume that as they enter this new arena of womanhood in life, things people and life itself will automatically make their dreams come true.

Many assume this because growing up as little girls in daddy or mummy's house often times were treated as little *'delicate flowers'* more than boys. So with this kind of care, perception and upbringing, the little girl grows to become *"a woman,"* still thinking that life and other things will be treating her at each level of her development, as a *"little delicate flower."*

Women are still delicate, but I wish in real adult life, this would stay the same as babyhood. Unfortunately, the more you grow in life the more one recognizes that skills are needed at each phase of development in order to stay relevant to your world. In view of the twists and turns in life, that little girl is all of a sudden, surrounded with complications of consistent demands and challenges of life as they grow into womanhood.

I therefore highly recommend this book, a functional wisdom with sound expository presentation, to the woman of the 21st century who desires to be successful in all aspects of life.

These wisdom principles set forth in this book, an expository of *Proverbs 31:10-31*, is a must to have for every woman. Frankly, excuse and ignorance which hinders productivity, both in the married and corporate world, has become obsolete and a liability in our modern world and its operations. Therefore everyone is looking anywhere at any price for the best to join their dream team.

So modern *"Woman,"* arm yourself with the wisdom loaded in this material so that value will be placed on your head everywhere you go in life.

Rev. Dr. Alex K. Mfum
Senior Pastor of Redemption Christian Center Intl.
Worcester, Massachusetts
USA.

FOREWORD IV

I must say I am privileged to write a foreword to this special write up on the *'Virtuous Woman.'* For many years I have given talks on marriage and shared in seminars whose panel included lawyers, doctors and lay people on the subject of marriage. In all these talks we highlighted on the virtuous woman as the woman who can make it in marriage. The virtuous woman in her wisdom is able to build her home and make it stand for her husband, children and even her housemaids.

Yes, our mother Eve failed to experience this after the enemy attacked her. However, the virtuous woman sees life in a very positive way and makes up her mind to use all her gifts to her advantage. She is determined to build her house on a solid rock. She sees the best of everything and works towards the goal she has set for herself and her household. The virtuous woman who diligently seeks the welfare of her husband is a great example for every married woman. Her aim is to win her husband's heart and to work to lift her husband up. She is determined to make it work. She did not see life as difficult but she broke through the difficulties of life and made her household happy.

The virtuous woman stands for the good church of today, a church that seeks the welfare of her members and builds them up into the full stature of Christ. She represents the church whose ministers, leaders and stewards, all team up to build the body of Christ and also ventures out to seek the welfare of the nation.

The church that plans and makes concrete programs to solve the needs of her people. The church that strives to eliminate nominalism and makes sure that the salvation message has reached every member of the church. Our mother Eve let us down and brought calamity on all of us.

But we can give praise to God our Father because He

"So loved the world that He gave His only begotten Son that whosoever believes in Him should not perish but have everlasting life." (John 3:16)

We still have to protect our position of grace through prayer since the threat continues to be real even as

"our enemy, the devil is roaring like the lion seeking whom he can devour." (I Peter 5:8)

We in the church should have the aim and determination of the virtuous woman. We should care about life and the things of God. I believe church people should set good examples.

It is time for both men and women to study the virtuous woman as described in *Proverbs 31:10-31*. It is applicable to any situation where there are relationships.

"Charm is deceitful and beauty is passing but a woman who fears the Lord, she shall be praised."(Proverbs 31:30).

Dr. Kate Lutterodt, a minister of God, has been a faithful member of the Kumasi Ministers' fellowship where my husband and I are also members. She looked up to us as parents and shared her dreams, upsets and joys with us. As a minister in the Oasis of Love International Worship Center, Kumasi, Ghana she was working with the children, young females preparing for marriage and Women Ministry.

She also taught Sunday school in addition to other church and pastoral duties. She has talked at seminars to various women's groups.

Dr. Lutterodt is a practical, down to earth, committed Christian. She always desires to share positively with others. I am extremely glad that the series of seminars she gave to enhance the lives of women has developed into this book.

It is my prayer this will be a best-selling book which will definitely enrich people's lives for decades.

Mrs. Victoria Brew Riverson
President of Ministers Wives Association and
Evangelist of Methodist Church Kumasi, Ghana.

FOREWORD V

Purity is a Commandment for Your Own Good

We live in a time where technology, exotic lifestyle, immense promiscuity, godlessness and so much more affect our lives, making it very difficult to live in holiness and purity as a single person and even as married couples.

Our selfish and godless ways has led to many evils and social vices such as unwanted pregnancies, leading to abortions, divorce and dysfunctional families and all forms of detestable sexual practices such as homosexuality and lesbianism.

The United States still has the highest rate of teen pregnancy and births in the industrialized world. Each year almost 750,000 teenage women aged 15-19 become pregnant. Eight out of ten of these pregnancies are unintended and 81% are to unmarried teens. A report by 'Save the Children', found that annually 13 million children are born to women under age 20 worldwide.

It is interesting to know that about two-thirds of births to teenage girls in the United States are fathered by men age 20 and over. Studies indicate that most of these girls are coerced or forced into sexual relations by older men who are supposed to know better.

Sex before marriage has become the norm instead of the exception in our world today.

One fifth of girls will have sex before the age of 13. In 2005, 47% of high school students (grades 9-12) reported ever having had sexual intercourse. Fourteen percent of high school students reported four or more sexual partners in 2005.

Dysfunctional families are continuously increasing; the divorce rate is tripling in numbers even in the Church.

God and His word have been replaced by humanism, self-ishness, uncleanness and detestable sexual behaviors. Let's consider what the Word of God say concerning these issues.

In 1Cor.6: 18-20 Paul states: "Flee fornication. Every sin that a man doeth is without the body, but he that commits fornication sinneth against his own body.
What? Know ye not that your body is the temple of the Holy Ghost, which is in you, which ye have of God, and ye are not your own? For ye are bought with a price: therefore glorify God in your body and in your spirit which are God's."

Thess.4: 7 "For God has not called us unto uncleanness but unto holiness."

Prov.5: 3-5 "For the lips of a strange woman drop as honey-comb, and her mouth is smoother than oil: but her end is bitter as wormwood, sharp as a two-edge sword. Her feet go down to death; her steps take hold on hell."

Lev. 20: 13 "If a man lies with a man as one lies with a woman, both of them have done what is detestable. They must be put to death; their blood will be on their own heads."

From the above scriptures and many more we deduce that God expects us to be holy. Sexual sins affect a person's body, soul and spirit. We all know the untold hardships that sexual sins have caused in our world today. Many marriages are destroyed due to unfaithfulness in the relationships. This has led to many dysfunctional families and all the child delinquencies that result from broken homes. As much as these social vices affect the core family, it also affects the society and the government as a whole.

*Teen pregnancy cost*s *the United States at least $7 billion annually.*

As a healthcare worker, I have witnessed some of the many diseases that individuals incur as a result of sexual promiscuity. Apart from the fact that this is a sin that affects your spirit and soul according to the word of God, it also in no doubt affects your physical body. Sexually Transmitted Diseases (STDS) cost the health care system a lot of money. The deadliest among these is **HIV/AIDS**.

The AIDS disease is deadly and is caused by the HIV virus. This virus is passed from one person to another through blood-to-blood contact and through sexual contact mostly. The AIDS infection is often severe and sometimes fatal. This is because the HIV virus ravages the immune system; hence the body's ability to fight sickness becomes highly compromised.

SOME AIDS CASES

*According to the CDC–Center for Disease Control, an estimated **850,000–950,000** persons in the United States are living with Human Immunodeficiency Virus (HIV), including **180,000-280,000** who do not know they are infected.*

*At the end of 2003, an estimated **1,039,000 to 1,185,000** persons in the United States were living with HIV/AIDS.*

*In 2005 **37,331** cases of HIV/AIDS in adults, adolescents and children were diagnosed in 33 States.* **From 2001 through 2005, the estimated number of persons in the 50 states and D.C living with AIDS increased from 331, 482 to 421,873- an increase of 27%.**

*In 2005, blacks (including African Americans) that make up approximately **13%** of the US population accounted for almost half of the estimated number of HIV/AIDS cases diagnosed.* **In 2005, the largest estimated proportion to HIV/AIDS diagnoses were men who have sex with men, followed by adult and adolescents infected through heterosexual contact.**

In 2007, an estimated 33.2 million persons worldwide are living with HIV. *Center for Disease Control and Prevention- CDC, has estimated **40,000** persons in the United States become infected with HIV each year.*

Deaths due to AIDS

The number of deaths from AIDS in 2007 is expected to total 2.1 million. Everyday over 6800 persons become infected with HIV and 5700 persons die from AIDS. The HIV pandemic remains the most serious of infectious disease challenges to public health.

From the above statistics we see the number of lives that this disease is affecting. There are other sources of contracting the HIV/AIDS virus, such as health care workers being exposed to infected blood and children who are born by infected mothers.

Of all the different sources, sexual exposure is the highest cause for HIV/AIDS. The lives that are ruined, family members that are devastated by the disease and death of loved ones, including the cost of health care to the nation cannot be overemphasized.

We need to protect ourselves from this deadly disease and all the hardships that ensue from illicit sexual behaviors. *People who are not married should avoid casual sex and let abstinence be their code of conduct, also married couples should be faithful and committed to each other.* A virtuous woman should not be ignorant of these facts.

This throws a great challenge to mothers to stand up to their responsibility of protecting, guarding and teaching the young ones. Even though the adult age is 18 years and children have the right to be independent and take their own decisions, issues pertaining to sex and marriage relationships are very complex and challenging. That one needs all the counseling and advice they can get.

I encourage the youth to be more discreet, patient, teachable and submissive to godly parental guidance in such issues.

The consequences of premarital-sex and immoral sexual sins are so enormous and devastating than the short-lived *"supposed sexual pleasure"*. Some of these consequences are; heart breaks, disappointments, leading to depression and many more emotional and physical ailments. We should not forget that sexual sin is the *one sin* that is done against one's own body, giving the devil the permission to destroy you.

Hence obedience to the word of God regarding sexual purity is beneficial to individuals and the society as a whole. As you live a life of purity you will save yourself from all the negative consequences mentioned above.

I encourage *everyone* to be committed to living a life of *Purity* whether married or not married and also encourage others to do the same.

I recommend the book, *'The Virtuous Woman'* to all.

God bless you as you read and strive to live according to the godly principles set forth in this book; for your physical, emotional and spiritual well being.

(Sources of statistical data: Center for Disease Control and Prevention- www.cdc.gov. Teen Pregnancy Prevention: Facts sheet. www.teenpregnancy.org)

By Miss Eva Bedford-Oppong (RN – BSN) Co-Author.

INTRODUCTION

In Genesis, we learn of the creation of the world [the heavens and the earth] the planetary systems and inhabitants: Vegetations, marine life, mammals, amphibians, fowls of the air and other living creatures. Adam (man) was the first human being to be created. He was alone. The creation of woman (Eve) was not an afterthought of God. He had a plan and purpose for mankind, and as we understand Him, through the Blessed Holy Trinity, is by definition in *"relationship."* So the creation of humanity is an extension of God's desire to be in relationship with man, who should also worship and reverence Him.

Matt 22:37-39 "Love the Lord your God with all your heart and with all your soul and with all of your mind. And love your neighbor as yourself."

God saw it was not good for man to be alone.

Gen 2:18 "And God said it is not good that man should be alone, I will make him a helpmate comparable to him."

So the first woman was formed to help, support, and compliment the first man to accomplish the task; to partner in ruling, increase, multiply, fill and subdue the earth (generational succession). The woman was created in a special way. She was a rib-bone from man, which was formed into a beautiful and wonderful being.

She was "*SEALED UP*" to ensure divine protection and security of womanhood. The woman was blessed and

endowed with glory, honor, authority and talents (ability) to be effective and beneficial to God and mankind (society at large).

Precious one, you are blessed to be reading this book. I was inspired by the Holy Spirit to put these important godly principles together, for women aspiring to be virtuous;

To share a testimony of my life and also to give insight into the goodness and mercies of our Lord and Savior Jesus Christ and the agape love He has for us all.

[Especially for women, emphasis mine] Let me share with you a short excerpt of this testimony to encourage you.

My Testimony of the 'un-aborted' baby.

At the age of 22 years I got pregnant and had my first child out of the wedlock. I had not made any preparation towards marriage and was not ready to raise a family.

Confused and desperate not knowing what to do with my self and the pregnancy, I tried my best to abort this child with doses of medications [21 tablets] even though 7 tablets was supposed to be enough to do the job together with some injections, but I did not succeed in my plan of abortion.

The pregnancy was about 21 days old. I tried staying away from church or any public gathering to avoid any embarrassment, and the fear of being recognized by anybody.

Can you imagine how one would feel in such situation?

But God in His infinite mercy and kindness revealed it to a prophetess in the church who called and told me all that was going on with me, to my surprise and amazement. She advised me to stop my plan of abortion for the Lord had told her to let me know that the child would be a great person, a blessing and support in future. The shock was too great to doubt or pursue the abortion, so I stopped.

Thus, with 21-days of pregnancy and 21 tablets ingested, she prayed that all the medications should rather make the baby strong.

I give praise and glory to the Almighty God today that the devil did not succeed in persuading me to destroy or kill [abort] my precious baby. Friends, had God not revealed this what do you think would have happened to the baby and me?

Well, at that time though it was a shameful, disappointing and heartbreaking incident, since there was no marriage out of that union, *but* the joy of having this wonderful baby fore-told by God, demands my gratitude to Him and great testimonies to share. The Lord also delivered me from the adulterous relationship and healed me from sicknesses of which doctors had given me 3 months to live. Praise God for that.

I strongly believe without a doubt that there are millions of women especially the youth who may be, or are guilty of this evil deed. We must all know, understand and accept first of all that this is evil; God hates and abhors abortion. Secondly you may be aborting your future blessing just as I was about to do, save the divine intervention of God.

I pray that if you or any one you know of [friends or relations] is anticipating having an abortion to *prayerfully* give it a second thought. Since abortion is sin against the command, divine purpose and handiwork of God. Not to mention the physical and emotional agonies associated with it.

Abortion, Is It a Woman's Right or Sin?
Check these scriptures:

Psalm. 127:3 "Lo, children are a heritage from the Lord; and the fruit of the womb is His reward."

Pregnancy can be explained to be the *fruit* of the womb from the Lord. It does not matter what stage or how old the fetus might be, *that clot of blood* is still a live *seed* from a man's *semen* in combination with a *live egg* from a woman in the maturing process to become a grown live *fruit* of the womb (A living being). Termination of this growing life is *murder*. Murder, [killing] is against God's word: the sixth of the Ten Commandments:

Exodus 20:13: "Thou shalt not kill."

*Hosea 4:2: "by swearing, lying, and **killing** and stealing and committing adultery, they break out and **blood** toucheth **blood**"*

Shedding of innocent blood is evil.

*Rev 22:14-15 "blessed are they that do his commandments that they may have the right to the tree of life, and may enter in through the gates into the city. For without are the dogs, and sorcerers and whoremongers, and **murderers** and idolaters and whosoever maketh a lie."*

Murderers including those who have abortion and do not repent and seek forgiveness will not enter the kingdom of heaven. However do not condemn yourself or feel rejected if you are guilty of this offence for that's the reason for the death of Christ. The *blood of JESUS* is always available to forgive, wash, purge and make you more 'precious than gold'.

Abortion therefore is biblically wrong, a sin and not a woman's right.

The "un-aborted baby's" graduation brought me to the *U.S.A.* She has indeed been a great blessing. She is *Eva,* the co-author of this book and partners with me as the vice-president of my ministry, *The Virtuous Woman Counseling and Outreach Ministry, which is a non-profit organization.*

After that episode I was presented with the opportunity to get married. Unfortunately again, I was ignorant of the godly principles of marriage. I agreed to become the second wife to a married man. In the beginning everything was fine but later, the pain and heartbreak was more than I can share with you in this book.

Amidst all of these, God blessed me with four more wonderful children. I am very grateful to God for my children, and very proud of them.

It was through all of this that Lord lifted me out '*gave me beauty for ashes*', and a ministry to women.

Precious one, I know your pain and heartbreak. I have been through it all. Years of rejection, loneliness, divorce, disappointment, failures, pain and shame in womanhood. God in His kind mercies has delivered me. He has sanctified, taught and prepared me as a blessing to you. Jesus has *healed and restored* me.

This is part of my numerous testimonies to the praise, thanksgiving and the glory of our God.

I therefore write this book to give you an insight of the valued and treasured gifts God has placed in a woman. Also that mothers and young women to be alert and make frantic effort to stop and discourage pre-marital sex which sometimes lead to teenage and unwanted pregnancies,

leading at times to abortion and also any form of adulterous relationship.

Hosea 4:6 "My people are destroyed for lack
of knowledge because: thou hast rejected knowledge,
I will also reject you…"

Women have missed the mark in many ways:

We have not come to the realization of our god-given status, potentials, and the responsibilities. Not to mention the precious valuable gifts that God has placed inside us.

"*The Virtuous Woman*," this wonderful material you hold is a special gift and *rhema* from God to help encourage and mold you into being the **excellent** woman, more precious than rubies to God, your husband, children, church and society at large.

Beloved get the knowledge of God so that you do not perish.

"God bless you **precious, virtuous woman**".

CHAPTER ONE

THE MYSTERY OF WOMANHOOD

WOMAN: Who is she?

Biologically: a woman is the female counterpart of man, *"sealed up."*

Biblically: she is the rib bone of man (Adam) formed into a being as his helpmeet. Gen. 2:22.

Spiritually: Woman is the bride of Christ.

The Bride of Christ:

2 Cor11: 2 "For I am jealous over you with a godly Jealousy, for l have espoused you to one husband that I may present you as a chaste virgin to Christ"

Isaiah 54:5 "For your Maker is your husband the Lord Almighty is His Name."

The relationship between husband and wife is similar to that between Christ and His church.

Eph 5:25 "Husbands love your wives as Christ also loved the church and gave himself for it. That he might sanctify and cleanse it with the washing of water by the word."

Rom.7: 4 "Wherefore, my brethren ye also are dead to the law by the body of Christ; that ye should be married to another, even to Him who was raised from the dead, that we should bring forth fruit unto God."

Woman is the bride of Christ owing to the relationship in which Christ stands for His church as Her husband.

We are said to be married to Christ so that we may bring forth fruit unto God. [*Rom.7: 4*]

This fruit, when opened releases the Holy Seeds, God's word, which has the power to save the souls unto Him. These souls shall be accounted to Him unto all generations.

Jesus Christ is the church maker by whom the Woman (the Church) is formed into a people. He (Christ) is the

Redeemer of the church by whom She (the Church) is bought out of captivity from the bondage of sin, which is the worst slavery.

The woman stands for the church, which Christ loved and gave Himself for Her to be holy, cleansing Her with water, which is His word.

The First Fruit of God:

James 1:18 "He chose to give us birth through the word of the truth that we might be a kind of first fruits of all he created."

A true Christian is someone who is born again and has become a completely new person from what he was before, by the renewing influence of the Holy Spirit and divine grace. By virtue of the grace and mercy of God, every Christian is the first fruit unto God. First fruit, in that he is God's portion and treasure and a peculiar property to Him, just as first fruits were to God in the Old Testament.

✱ *Ex. 23: 19 "Bring the best of the first fruits of your soil to the house of the Lord your God."*

> **Become holy and consecrated to the Lord just as the first fruits are consecrated to Him. Christ is the first fruit of God sacrificed for Christians. Christians are therefore expected to be first fruits unto God.**

✓ We are to present ourselves as living sacrifice, best price, clean, with the status of the *"pure original state."* This is a kind of *"spiritual virginity."*

Rev 14 4: "These are those who do not defile themselves with men or women: For they are virgins. They were purchased from among men and offered as first fruits unto God and to the Lamb."

> **This is plain evidence of the special redemption of Christ. For they are virgins, they have not defiled themselves with carnal or spiritual adultery; they kept themselves pure from the abomination of anti-Christian generation.**

They are virgins by their loyalty and steadfast adherence to Christ. These Christians follow the law and the conduct of God's word in spirit and in truth, leaving their desires to Him, to lead them into whatever He requires them to do regardless of the challenges that they may encounter.

Their desire is to please their Lord.

As a good dedicated Christian, you are one of these virgins. Consider and cherish the fact that you have been espoused to Christ and so you ought to live a life that pleases Him. You need to stay holy and righteous.

Remember that God fearfully and wonderfully made you. That is why as a woman in Christ, you should be motivated to live your life in holiness and purity to the glory of God.

THE PURE ORIGINAL STATE

Virtuous: derives from the word *virtue*.

It implies: moral excellence, righteousness, goodness and rectitude (correct behavior in accordance to uprightness).

It also means strength, chaste (chastity), especially of a woman.

That is to be morally pure, modest, celibate, abstaining from sexual intercourse (until marriage).

Virtue is derived from the word *Virgin.*

It means to be in a *pure* and *natural*, of the *original state*. Simply put, a virgin, one who has never known a man.

Examples of women in the Bible who were virgins: The Blessed Virgin Mary, Esther, Rachel and Rebecca.

These women of virtue were blessed and highly favored in their marital, childbearing and other aspects of their lives.

It is indeed worthy and graceful to preserve your virginity as a young woman till you get married.

However, even if you have lost your **virginity,** you can still become a **virtuous woman; maintain a 'second virginity'** as you apply the biblical principles in this book so you can be blessed and highly favored of God.

The Mystery of Womanhood

The mystery of the woman is her *"Virginity"* or her *"Sealed state"*. God in His divine wisdom and power took a rib bone from Adam (man) and in the process of the

formation of a woman, *"sealed"* her up with a thin membrane, an organ consisting of *"Blood"* called the *"Hymen"* a Latin word which comes from Greek word *"humen"* meaning **membrane.**

Hymen is a Greek mythology meaning, *"the god of marriage."*

Understand that only in marriage should the husband break the hymen of the woman.

This seal in the form of hymen signifies a woman's dignity, pride, integrity, chastity, purity, indeed her glory and honor. Nothing or no one can break or tamper with this sacred thing without an act of entrance into a woman through sexual intercourse of course, by a man. It cannot also be broken without **blood** being **spilled.**

A **blood covenant** is thereby established. God *"sealed"* women up to ensure maximum protection, security, respect, honor and the dignity of womanhood.

Also as a living sacrifice, a vessel of honor sanctified for the master's use.

2 Cor. 11:2-3 "I am jealous for you with a godly jealousy, I promised you to one Husband; so that I might present you a pure virgin to Him."

Paul said he wanted you to be presented to Christ as a pure virgin. This presentation begins with how you live a life pure and spotless here on the earth; guiding your mind against false doctrines, not as Eve who was beguiled by the subtlety of the serpent. Holy living is the absence of a proposed sin. You know what I am saying? Every act of sin is planned, and it is in stages. Everyone who is tempted to sin has the grace period to reconsider the act and resist the temptation. In other words there is no excuse for sinning.

When you get born again, a blood covenant is established through the blood of Jesus, which was shed before the foundation of the world. The conversion of a soul is its marriage *[entering into a close union with]* to the Lord Jesus Christ. *(Isaiah 54:5)*

When we receive the Holy Spirit baptism we get the ***seal*** of our salvation and ***guarantee*** as children of God and heirs to the throne.

In fact the Holy Spirit is a ***seal***.

When a woman's virginity or the **'seal'** is broken, a blood covenant is also established between the man and the woman involved.

This is a ***mystery*** concerning the ***sex act*** between the man and the woman; hence, a new life begins. So it is that a woman should begin a new life immediately the "***hymen***" is broken by the husband,[a new life of bonded unity] which goes with a blood covenant after a ***blessed marriage***.

A woman's hymen has been fastened as a seal to ***guarantee the authenticity*** or proof of her womanhood, pride and integrity making it secure against ***illegal*** entrance.

Breaking of this seal establishes a strong bond (soul-tie).

Such bonded unity cannot easily be broken; it is so sacred, perfect and beautiful in the sight of God.

The significance of the bloodshed after consummation [sexual intercourse] in marriage or outside of marriage would be discussed later in chapter 8 - "***Sex the strongest human covenant.***"

I would like us to discuss the word '***Seal***'
Webster's dictionary: ***Seal*** *means guarantee, pledge.*
- Something that seals or close up.
*-To **authenticate**, to **fasten** to **prevent tampering**, to close*
*or **secure** against access [illegal] leakage or **passage**.*

Know that you are God's temple and that the Spirit of Christ is in you. Get me right that the Holy Spirit is in you to assist you in many ways including every decision you make in the now and also to convict you of your sins.

Likewise the Holy Spirit ***guarantees*** your salvation, ***authenticates*** you as a child of God and heirs to the heavenly throne ***pledges*** His comfort and power, prevents and ***secures*** you against the ***access*** of the enemy.

*Eph. 1:13 "And you also were included in Christ when you heard the word of truth, the gospel of your salvation. Having believed you were marked in Him with a **seal**, the promised Holy Spirit."*

God wants us to live a healthy life. He wants His temple to become clean, ***holy***, sanctified and acceptable to Him.

1 Cor 3:16 "Don't you know you are God's temple and that God's Spirit lives in you? Whosoever destroys the temple of God would be destroyed."

A married woman's virginity was celebrated in the Old Testament:

Deut 22:13-21 have the laws concerning chastity /virginity.

This section of scripture deals with the laws of proper sexual conduct.

Violations were punishable by stoning violators to death.

'Tokens of the damsel's virginity' refer to those means by which a betrothed woman's family proved her virginity to the husband's family and elders of the town.
A white bed-cloth is supposed to be stained with blood on the honey moon night.

Deut. 22:16-18 "The girl's father will say to the elders, I gave my daughter in marriage to this man, but he dislikes her, now he has slandered her and said. I did not find your daughter to be a virgin. But here is proof of my daughter's virginity: Then her parents shall display the cloth before the elders of the town, and the elders shall take the man and punish him."

Read about the 400 virgins who were saved in *Judges 21:11, 12*

Societies' Restrictions about Sex

Even primitive societies that have never heard the Gospel of Jesus Christ imposes some limitations on sexual conduct. In fact, all known societies have regulated sex in some way, either with written customs and taboos.

This shows we human beings know, deep down inside, that sex is a very important and serious matter.

In Muslim countries, every unmarried woman must wear a veil to conceal her beauty from any men she might meet on her village. The enjoyment of a woman's charms is a privilege reserved for her husband alone. In Ancient China, the parents of a boy chose his bride while he was still a child, but the youngsters were not allowed to see one another until their wedding day.

Why? - To preserve their sexual purity. Indians including other nationalities observe similar customs and traditions.

Anthropologists have found similar laws and customs in every known society, both ancient and modern. Many of these communities have never heard of God, and certainly had never read the Bible yet they knew by instinct that they should safeguard the dignity of sex. They knew it should be protected and used for the right purpose- within marriage.

As mothers and fellow Christian women we have a big task in:

Titus 2:3-5: "The aged women likewise, that they be in behavior as becometh holiness, not false accusers, not given to much wine, teachers of good things."

Paul is saying that the aged women should ensure the maintenance of young ladies' welfare and purity. They should have concern to uphold the future reputation of the young women since they are the branches for posterity.

As a young lady, you also have the right and responsibility to preserve your virginity. That is your honor; it is your life, pride, integrity and your value. You should make every effort, and pay every price to keep your virginity for the god-sent man.

I would like to caution men here that the woman stands for the church as the bride of Christ. So whatever abuse, dishonor or shame meted out to a woman is done to the church. And Jesus will judge anyone who destroys or pulls down His bride, the church.

Consider the new birth in Christ. The spirit of a man gets born again, after the Holy Spirit has convinced him, and regeneration has taken place. So the man becomes a new person in Christ. This experience connects him to the Spirit of God; hence he becomes a joint heir with Christ. But his soul, the mental sphere of him must be exposed to the things of God. That is to say that his mental sphere, his mind or the soul must be cleansed through the word of God.

Understand that the entrance of God's word gives light. This word of the Lord works on the mind, through the godly principles to bring about the transformation of the entire being, the human body.

So we need the Holy Spirit to strengthen us in our efforts to get good information that is capable of bringing about the change.

Be encouraged in the redemptive work of our *Lord Jesus Christ,* that if you have in any way lost your *pure original state or* **virginity** *the precious blood of Jesus is available to cleanse, wash and sanctify you and 'lock' you up again and accept you as His bride.*

Make every effort to maintain your deliverance!

RAPE CASES: A Capital Offence

Rape is a force to have sexual intercourse against the victim's will. This is another form of evil that is meted to women mostly, during which one's virginity is broken. Rapists were punished by death in the Bible:

Deut. 22; 25-27 "But if a man finds a virgin/damsel in the field and the man force her and lies with her then the man only that lay with her shall die.

But unto the damsel you shall do nothing; there is in the damsel no sin worthy of death; for as a man riseth against his neighbor, and slayeth him, even so is this matter. For he found her in the field, and the betrothed damsel cried, and there was none to save her."

How many victims of rape have cried in pain and desperation with no one to help, and sometimes with no one to share their pains and heartbreaks? Some of them have to live with the emotional trauma for life.

This evil act has been of old because the devil has been busy with evil since the beginning of creation.

Even in the Old Testament times, one of the sexual perversions that dehumanize the self-image of women was rape, a very sinful and demonic act. It always seems to be covered up due to its shamefulness and offensiveness.

Rape is one of the most heinous crimes imaginable that can be done to a person mostly women, girls (and sometimes boys) and even some at a very young age.

The Bible admonishes us to be wise and careful not fools.

Eph 5:15 "See then that ye walk circumspectly not as fools, but as wise redeeming the time for the days are evil"

Women, especially young ladies must refrain from provocative dresses and immoral activities, since it does not glorify God neither does it bring honor to your moral integrity and self-image.

The devil that was thrown down on this earth since creation is still at work in diverse ways, to steal, destroy and kill the image, purity, chastity and the moral *integrity* of women, just as he did to Eve in the Garden of Eden; stole her joy, destroyed her relationship with God and brought eternal death on her and Adam.

Both all the unrighteous, innocent and good people become victims. Most often the offenders may get away unseen or unpunished.

But it is possible for the wicked to prosper and the righteous be person to suffer. But the truth is God assures us that the end of the wicked is total destruction.

Sometimes, He may punish them immediately or later but their punishment will surely come.

That is why parents, guardians and Christian leaders should be alert and more protective over the moral activities of their young ladies giving those who may be victims all the support they need.

Rape is a matter of the heart, mind and emotions.

That is why the victim cannot be comforted, appeased and restored easily through '*mere*' words. I love to tell, that lady, who has been through the agony of rape or defilement that Jesus is real and can comfort and heal *yes!*

He can restore you in a way that no one else can.

Jesus can cleanse you and fill you with His love, peace and confidence. Trust Him as God, who washes, purifies and cleanses our sins, and restores us.

Ps. 103:1-5 "Bless the Lord oh my soul and all that is within me, bless his holy name. Bless the Lord, oh my soul and forget not all his benefits: who forgives all your iniquities. Who heals all your diseases, who redeems your life from destruction. Who crowns you with loving kindness and tender mercies, who satisfies your mouth with good things, so that your youth is renewed like the eagle's."

Surrender to Him today, your heart, mind and emotions, your anger, helplessness, frustrations, questions, and your condemnation and trust Him to restore you. Jesus Christ is well able to give you the peace and happiness your heart so need and desire. Only surrender your all to Him now!

Do not suffer in pain and silence *speak out* seek counseling from a certified Christian counselor. The prayer keys in chapter 9 can be helpful.

CHAPTER TWO

CREATION OF WOMAN AND ITS SIGNIFICANCE

WHERE AND WHEN WAS WOMAN CREATED

The original home or birthplace of Eve was very pleasant and glorious, the Garden of Eden, where God had already formed and placed Adam.

The word Eden in the Hebrew language implies delight and pleasure.

Given the literal meaning, the Garden of Eden was a place hedged round or protected, a delightful shelter, containing what the man needed. The description of the Garden of Eden is in detail later in the chapter.

Now the formation of Adam;

*Gen 2:7 "And the Lord God formed man **of the dust of the ground and** breath into his nostrils the breath of life; and man became a living soul."*

The planting of Eden and the placing of Adam;

Vs. 8; and the Lord God planted a garden eastward in Eden; and there he put the man whom he had formed.

The provision in Eden made for pleasure and food for Adam:

Gen 2:9a "and out of the ground made the Lord God to grow every tree that was pleasant to sight and good for food....".

From the above we learnt the man Adam was made out of paradise and after God had formed him, He put him into the Garden. This shows that Adam was made out of common clay not of the paradise-dust. He lived *outside* of Eden before he *lived in it that* he might see that all the comforts of his paradise-state were owing to God's free grace.

Adam could not claim a tenant–right to the garden, for he was not formed upon the premises nor had anything of his own but what he received from God right in the garden. Human boasting was hereby forever excluded.

God made us out of nothing and placed us into a place of honor and abundance. All is just by *His grace* that is why no one should boast of anything he has acquired. It's all by grace.

The creation of the woman (details in the following chapter)

Gen 2:21 "And the rib, which the Lord God the man made he a woman, and brought her to the man."

The woman was created after Adam had been transferred from the common dust into the paradise *state*.

We can say then that Eve was a citizen of paradise, implying the woman was formed on the premises of Eden, a place of delight, pleasure and honor.

Adam was formed outside the paradise; Eve [woman] was formed inside the premises of paradise. So women, see for yourselves where God formed you and praise God.

The man was **dust** refined but the woman was **dust double** refined, one remove further from the earth.

Let us now examine briefly the residence or the palace of Adam and Eve–the Eden of God. The place appointed for Adam's residence was a *"garden."* It was not an ivory house or a place overlaid with gold, but a garden furnished and adorned by nature.

Adam and Eve lived in innocence. So they need no stately decorated and magnified building. Their clothes were simply the glory of God. The heaven was the roof of Adam's house. There has never been any roof so curiously sealed and painted. The earth was the floor, never was any floor richly laid out.

The shadow of the trees was his retirement and under those trees were his dinning rooms and lodging. And never again was any room finely hung as these.

Solomon in all his wisdom was not arrayed like this.

It is therefore better if we accommodate ourselves to plain things. The less we indulge ourselves with these artificial delights which have been invented to gratify man's pride and luxury, the nearer we will approach to a state of innocence and content. Adam and Eve were content with their environment.

Nature is content with little and that which is most natural. Grace is content with less but lust with nothing. The device and furniture of this garden was the immediate work of God's wisdom and power.

This was '**Where**' Eve was created.

When? She was created on the 6th day of creation.

Genesis 1:13b "so the evening and the morning were the 6th day"

Just think of God's wisdom, manifold blessing and abundant provision; a well-prepared place first for Adam

Gen 2:15 "And the Lord God took the man, and put him in the Garden of Eden to dress and keep it".

*Adam was to posses, work and **maintain** the garden to be fruitful a place for Eve's comfort.*

Men ought to provide a befitting accommodation for their wives, even before the arrival of their brides.

Virtuous women indeed do deserve it.

That was the situation of the residence of Adam and Eve, the Garden of Eden, signifying delight and pleasure...

Beloved let it be our care to secure a place in the heavenly paradise. Then we will not need to perplex ourselves with a search after earthly paradise, which *Eccl. 1:2 says "it is all vanity"*

HOW WAS THE WOMAN CREATED AND IT'S SIGNIFICANCE

We have learnt about, who a woman is, when and where she was created, and also how Adam was formed,

In this section we shall focus on how or the way and manner God chose to create a woman.

Of course, in a very unique and significant manner God portrays her likeness with Himself and oneness with man. Both Adam and Eve were made in the image of God to stand as God's perfect representatives on earth.

Gen 1:26-27 "Then God said let us make man in our own image and likeness. So God created man in his own image, in the image of God he created Him, male and female he created them".

God in His divine wisdom and power chose to create woman in a different way and manner and at a different time.

Genesis 2:21; "and the Lord God caused a deep sleep to fall on Adam and he slept. He took one of his ribs and closed up with flesh in its place.
Then the rib which the Lord God had taken from the man [Adam] he formed into a beautiful, wonderful being, woman and He brought her to man".

That was how the woman was formed. Let us consider the woman, who has been already formed from man or was part of man **but** in form of a rib bone.

Woman, in other words is *'womb-man'* is said to be in the *womb* of man (as a rib bone).

The word *"womb man"* also implies the ability and creative aspect of mankind.

1 Cor11: 8 "for the man is not from the woman but woman from the man."

There are three significant aspects of this mystery to be studied:

The 1st Significant Aspect of Eve's Creation.

That God caused a deep sleep on Adam while his wife was in the making.

This signifies that: Adam had no part to play in it. He did not join in the formulation of Eve. It was totally from God's own initiative. Adam took no counsel with God, nor did he direct the Holy Spirit his counselor in the act.

1. Adam slept soundly and sweetly as one who had all his cares cast on God.
2. Adam cheerfully and confidently resigned himself (body, soul, spirit) and his affairs to his maker's will and wisdom.
3. Understand that Jehovah Jireh, our Lord provides when and how, and to whom He pleases.
4. God will surely and graciously work for us and for our good.
5. That the opening of his side might be no grievance to him; while he knew no sin.

God surely cared, and he felt no pain. When God by His providence, does that to His people which is grievous to the flesh and blood, He not only consults our happiness in the issue, but by His grace can so quiet and compose our spirits, to make things easy under the sharpest and painful afflictions. His divine Grace will strengthen us, especially women even in our numerous severe agonies.

Adam lost a rib, and without any diminution or comeliness to his strength, [for, doubtless, the flesh was closed without a scar.] But in place of the rib, Adam was blessed with Eve, a helpmeet that abundantly made up for his loss, one more precious than rubies and greater than a rib-bone.

Whatever God takes away from our lives, He will one-way or the other increase and restore with advantage. Adam's surgery (the first surgery ever made) was without pain or a scar.

The 2nd Significant Aspect of Eve's Creation

The rib of man formed into a woman:
1. The divine closeness of man to woman.

2. The bond that is expected to exist between man and woman. *[What God has joined together let no man put asunder.]*
3. The woman was the reflection of man's glory, deriving *that **honor of man*** of whom she was made. This shows the reflection of man's glory and the best honor she *derives from man.*
4. Man is hereby mandated to love and respect the woman who was formed from his rib and is part of him.
5. The subjection and reverence that the wife owes to her own husband.
6. The man is the **head** of the family while the woman the **heart** of the family, remains the **crown of visible creation.** Woman, whose price is far above rubies, was a perfectly created being.
7. Hence the *uniqueness* of woman revealed.

The 3rd Aspect of Woman's Creation:
Adam's declaration of this is "the bone of my bones and flesh of my flesh."

1. The unity that God planned for man and woman.
2. The woman is inseparably link to man.
3. Unity of human race assured.
4. The woman's dignity, gracefulness and value are affirmed.
5. The foundation of Christian marriage is affirmed and set forth in a memorable way.

'This is':
Referring to the woman [Eve], implies her *surety or specifically* Adam's affirmation of his desire to have her.

(As *if to say, yes! that's exactly what I've been waiting for.)*

The **"Bone of my bone and flesh of my flesh;"**
Expresses the profound love and acceptance for the woman by the man.

The Hebrew word, "Ish" literally means man and "Ishash" referring to woman is an expression of blood relationship, equality and likeness in spirit, soul and body of man and woman.

[Adam's declaration sounds like; we are one, we are the same, and you are mine.]

Adam made another declaration: "*She shall be called woman.*" This signifies the naming of the woman, which will be studied later.

Women from creation are very precious and special to God and man (including Adam), uniquely formed and created. Beloved sister know this: you are specially made with an inestimable value and a price so dear:

Psalm 139:14 "We are fearfully and wonderfully made."

Be mindful of fact that you were created with glory, honor and dignity, and careful not to cast away your confidence. If by any means you have or feel abused, belittled, disgraced or lost your dignity and respect in any way, there is good news for you. Jesus restores and makes anew. The blood of Jesus is available to cleanse, purify, purge and adopt you as God's child again.

Due to your unique creation, and importance in life no matter your situation, failures or circumstances, the **value** upon your life cannot ever be changed or destroyed.

Come to Jesus.

Why was Woman Created?
This study is on why God created the woman. It will help you understand well God's plan and purpose for the woman towards man and creation.

Genesis 2:18; "And the Lord God said it is not good that man should be alone; I will make him a helper comparable to him."

Observe how God graciously adopted Adam's solitude. God as we understand Him through the doctrine of the Holy Trinity is by definition in relationship. This creation of humanity is an extension of God's desire to be in relationship with man.

Man was made just a little lower than the angels, with all other things under his domain.

Psalm 8: 4-6 "what is man, that thou visit him? For thou hast made him a little lower than the angels, and hast crowned him with glory and honor. Thou maddest him to have dominion over the works of thy hands; thou hast put all under his feet."

In the hierarchy of God's creation, there was no being of the same nature and rank with Adam whom he could communicate or familiarize with. He was truly lonely. God knew **what was good for Adam; that, it was not good** for Adam to be **alone.**

There must be a companion for his comfort, to provide for his physical, spiritual and emotional needs and well being. The woman was created as a **perfect counterpart** of man to be adoptable to him. God worked out His planned purpose and place for the woman on earth towards man and all His creation. It was a pleasure for Adam to exchange knowledge and affection to one of his own kind, to inform and be informed, to love and be loved.

Solomon said in *Eccl. 4:9-10* "*Two are better than one for they have good reward for their labor, for if they fall the one will lift up his fellow; but woe to him that is alone when he falleth for he hath not another to lift him up.*"

Imagine one man in the whole world! What a melancholy man he must have been!

A perfect solitude (a condition of isolation) would turn a paradise into a desert and a palace into a dungeon, without the woman.

God did not create man alone for the increase and continuance of his kind. He could have created a world of all men to replenish the earth.

The world, you can imagine, would have been too 'straight and boring' for the designed number of men to live together at once. So God in His divine wisdom saw it fit to make up that number of succession of generation.

Male and female will ever be one:

✱ ***Gen 1:8b*** "*I will make him a helper comparable or fit him.*"

Let us consider the word **helper** in Hebrew is *'ezer'*, which describes the **functions or fit** and can be translated to mean **equal and corresponding** to him. Men and women must marry their match and be **adoptable to each other.**

One who have the same nature and rank of being, help near him, one to co-habit with him, to be always at hand. A help before him, one that he could look upon with pleasure and delight to share his love, sorrow, joy, ideas and plans in life.

God's plan for **marriage** in *Gen 2: 2* was introduced and repeated in *Matthew 19:5* and *Eph 3:31*:

> *"Therefore a man shall leave his father and mother and cleave to wife and the two shall be one."*

Man made of spirit, soul and body has physical, emotional and spiritual needs which only another human of his kind could meet. The woman is an ultimate friend to man to bring comfort and good fellowship. The woman who was created as a perfect counterpart to man, is to assist him make up the succession to the generation unborn. That is to increase and multiply and fill the earth.

The woman's vital need for her creation was declared for Adam [man] cannot bear children alone.

Gen 1:28 "Be fruitful and multiply and fill the earth, subdue and have dominion over it."

God blessed mankind with honor, grace and ability by the authority and responsibility to be partners in ruling the earth through multiplication and fruitfulness. Indeed, God provided and backed His words with performance and productivity.

Be fruitful and multiply does not mean human reproduction alone but fruitfulness, multiplication in bearing good fruit in the kingdom business as the *vine* and its branches. [Soul winning]

The woman has a divine spiritual duty and obligation in the **kingdom; in and outside the church**, hence Women's Ministry is affirmed. *(Titus 2:3-5)*

The woman is inseparably linked to the man by her creation. The value and price of a fruitful woman affirmed in *Prov. 31:30.*

The woman's creation stands for the Christian marriage which reflects threefold miracle:

51

- **Biological**: That is two people have become one flesh. This is unity and love in sexual intimacy where another being or a child is born.
- **Social miracle**; two families grafted together.
- **Spiritual**: Marriage union that represents the union of Christ and His bride, the Church.

> **Therefore man is the Head, which is Christ and woman is the heart that is the Church.** *(Eph. 5:23-27).*

The creation of the woman was not an after thought of the creator; God executed His plan for both man and woman. The woman was created to accomplish and complete God's plan for mankind. Man needs a woman to make him complete so does the woman.

The woman could be said to be weak and incapable without man, in the accomplishment of her task of womanhood, motherhood and a times as a minister of the gospel, as the bride of Christ, the church.

Likewise the man needs a helpmeet to make him complete in his fatherhood, manhood, the high priest of the home, and also even in ministry.

For this reason, the best state in this world is that we have need of one another's help, since we are members of one body. We must therefore be glad to give and receive help from one another to enable us perform quality tasks as unto God.

THE EQUALITY OR PARITY OF MAN AND WOMAN AT CREATION

A woman in general, is looked down upon she could sometimes be treated with contempt and is not accepted in certain categories, of life especially in ministry.

The woman is said to be a weaker vessel in *nature and constitution*, and so need to be defended.

However, the woman *is in other higher respects equal to man* equality or parity of man and woman from creation is very important and does prove so. God's purpose for creating man and woman made us equal in "his own image *and likeness*."

There are two aspects to be considered. First, man and woman were like God:

Gen. 1:26a "let us make man in our own image and likeness."

Gen. 1:27, "so God created man in his own image, the image of God he created him; male and female, he created he them."

Gen. 2:22 continues as "then the Lord God made woman from the rib he had taken out from man and he brought her to the man."

Secondly, the man and the woman were without sin, so their nakedness was not shameful. The two were equally righteous before the Lord. Let us consider this, "let us make man in our image and likeness." By this we deduce that the three persons of the Holy Trinity, that is, God the father, God the son, and God the Holy Spirit consulted and agreed upon the creation of man. This indicates that man was made to be dedicated and devoted to God the Father, Son and the Holy Spirit.

Unto the great name we are all with good reason baptized. For that great name we owe our being. Let him (God) rule man who said, "let us make man."

When we analyze the two words *image and likeness* of God of which male and female (Adam and Eve) were made. Adam was not made in the likeness of any creature that went before him but in the **likeness** of his Creator. In the same **likeness** the woman (Eve) was created.

The Lord Jesus Christ is the only express image of God's person, as the only begotten son of His father having the same nature as God. When a man gets born again, the same honor in the nature of God is transferred on him. The same measure of honor is equally bestowed upon the woman who has turned her heart unto the Lord.

Understand the nature and the constitution of God but not of His body (for God has no physical body). God breathed into the nostrils of man and he [man] became a living soul. The *"living soul"* aspect of man has two spheres, the human spirit and the human soul. The human spirit of man connects him to God supernaturally speaking. It is also known as the likeness of God. The **soul** of a man is not his spirit, but the mental sphere of him.

This is the house of intelligence, the center of information and thoughts. It is also known as the **image** of God (or bears God's image.)

Consider the components of man, his spirit, soul and body. The body of man is the outward part of him. This is the envelope that carries the abdominal contents. Though the human body is the physical aspect of man, the flesh, yet has roles to play in establishing the purpose of the spiritual world on earth.

Prov. 20:27 "that the spirit of man is the candle
of the Lord"

God forms the spirit of man within him. It is a divine light; a candle of His lighting for is the inspiration of the Almighty that gives us understanding. This is a candle not only lighted by Him but also lighted for Him.

It is a discovering light by the help of reason we come to know men, to judge of their characters and dive into their designs, by the help of conscience we come to know ourselves.

The image of God in man is to enable him (man) to use his faculties of creativity through the use of the human mind. And the likeness of God in man is to enable him to live on earth as a representative of God.

Both male and female therefore were appointed governors and representatives of God on earth over other creatures. Man also is designated to reverence and fear God.

At creation God's image upon the male and female consists:

Of His *knowledge, righteousness and true holiness*. That was what enabled man and woman to be very upright, their consistent conformity with the supernatural world of God was within the will of God. All these good and honorable virtues were bestowed on our first parents.

The man and the woman had equal access to God's supernatural, provision flowing down through the natural realm into things relating to human and blood relationship. However the two, Adam and Eve had different functions. Both were blessed, honored, charged and provided with the divine ability, authority and power to produce and fill the earth to continue with creation, a generational succession and for the cause of the gospel.

Equality or parity of man and woman from creation is affirmed also in *Genesis 2:22* where the rib taken from Adam's side was used to form the woman. It is clear that the woman was not made out of Adam's head to *rule over* him, nor *out of his feet* for Adam to trample upon her. She was created *out of his side* to be *equal* with him. She was created *under his arm to be protected, near his heart to be loved*. Adam's rib, bone of his bone and flesh of his flesh makes them *equal* also in blood relationship.

Woman just like man consists of the body, soul and spirit.

A ***body*** made out of common dust
A ***rational immortal soul; the*** *breath of God;*
And ***spirit*** from the invisible Holy Spirit.

The man and the woman were made equal to reflect the body of Christ and the Church. Adam was a figure of Him who was to come, for out of the side of our Lord Jesus

Christ, the second Adam, His *spouse* the Church became manifest.

Check this: Adam's side was opened for a rib to form the woman, his bride. Likewise when Jesus slept on the cross and His side was pierced, water and blood came out. The blood was to purchase His [bride] Church and the water to purify Her.

The institution of marriage therefore is deep and indeed a mystery and must be respected and reverend as unto the Lord.

Eph 5: 25-26 "husbands love your wives just as Christ loved the church and have himself for her that he may sanctify and cleanse her with the washing of water by the word, that he might present her to himself a glorious church not having spot or wrinkle or any such thing but she may be holy without blemish."

That was how the equality of man and woman from creation established by the institution of marriage as compared with Christ and the Church.

The scripture below affirms man and woman's equality as heirs to the heavenly throne, so the woman is to be treated with love and respect:

1Peter 3:7 "Husbands in the same way are to be considerate as you live with your wives and treat them with respect as weaker vessels, partners and as joint heirs with you in the gracious gift of life, so that nothing will hinder your prayers."

✳Man and woman were created equal into the same *divine wisdom and immortal Spirit of* **God** They both have **God's understanding, will, knowledge and His active power.** Each having his own fundamental free *will.* Adam and Eve were equal in flesh, blood and spirit but with different important functions within each person according to each one's strength and capabilities.

The woman is equally empowered to carry out her own functions within her female capacity just as the man has the ability to carry out his own functions within his male capacity. Therefore the man should not look down on the woman as weak and inferior or incapable of doing great things especially in spiritual matters.

The man or the woman cannot speak evil of one or the other but show love and concern for each other in all things, showing mutual respect to one another according to the Word. Disrespect of the woman can hinder your prayers.

The Significance of Adam Naming Eve.

A name is the first *gift given to every newborn child.* Every living being needs and has a name. Names in most cultures are significant and in most cases do imply your origin, authority, and responsibility.

Names can even determine ones destiny. Names have meanings and people and places are named after certain things for a lot of reasons. Names more often than not have impact on lives in the negative, or in positive it may be a blessing or otherwise.

Adam's naming of Eve does not in itself '*mean total control or despotic*' over her but rather in token of his acceptance of Eve and accordance with the authority given him.

Genesis 2:23b, "she shall be called woman,
because she was taken out of man".

Adam in appreciation and recognition of Eve's origin, named her woman because she was part of his body.
Eve's name is therefore in recognition of her origin.

In Genesis 2:15, 20: God assigned Adam the authority and responsibility for the protection and provision of names for all creatures.

Gen. 2:15; "The Lord God took the man and put him in the Garden of Eden to work on it and take care of it".

Gen. 2: 20; "so the man gave names to all the livestock, the birds of the air and all the beast of the field."

Gen 3:20, 'Adam called his wife Eve because she was to become the mother of all the living'.

"*Eve*" in Hebrew literally means "*life*" or "*living*".
The word "***woman***" in Hebrew is "*Ishah*" and "*Man*" is "*Ish.*" This denotes blood relationship hence; Adam ***could*** claim ownership of the woman as his ***but*** this was an act of faith in God's promise.

God has dominion over Adam as a result of which He gave him the name Adam, which signifies "*Red earth*"; where he originated.

In the genealogy of dominion from God unto the man, Adam also named Eve, an evidence of his acceptance and godly authority over her. Nevertheless, Eve was to be the mother of all the living. Adam had before called his wife a woman. The word *"woman"* for *Eve*, coming from the word *"Ishah" also means "life"* or the mother of all living. Every woman is a wife and a mother. Now if Adam did the naming of Eve by divine direction, it was an act of God's favor.

Just like the direction of God's favor in the naming of Abraham and Sarah, as a seal of His covenant with them.

This was an assurance to the two of them that come what may, and their sin notwithstanding, together with the results of sin and God's displeasure against them; that God would keep his word, *"life,"* which was revealed in Eve's name. Eve brought in sin and death but her name *"life"* made the difference.

She was indeed the mother of the living. Hence, God would continue to bless them in the light of His proclamation, "be fruitful and multiply."

It was likewise a confirmation of the promise, which God made that the seed of Eve (life) should break the serpent's head. The woman Mary and her seed, Jesus should conquer Satan, sin and death.

Adam's naming of Eve himself was an instance of his faith in the word of God. It was also in humble confidence and dependence upon the blessing. However, God spared such sinners to be the parents of *all living*.

The blessing of a redeemer, the seed of the woman, in which Adam played very important roles in calling his wife Eve meaning life. For that redeemer shall be the life of all the living and in Him shall all this families of the earth be blessed. That is the significance of Adam naming Eve.

It is in order that the woman assumes the name of her spouse; hence forgo her paternal family name. This depicts belonging, authority and acceptance for both of them.

For example in *Gen 17: 3-8*

Abraham's renaming; from Abram to Abraham which made him *blessed* and a *father* of many nations and Sarai to Sarah also *blessed* and a *mother* of nations.

Gen 35: 10

Jacob the *sup planter* had his name changed to *Israel*.

Genesis 41:45

Joseph was renamed Zaphenath–Paneah by Pharoah confirming his *citizenship* and *authority* in Egypt.

2 Kings 24:17

The renaming of Mathaniah to Zedekiah by Nebuchadnezzar made him *king* in his place.

We can go on with the renaming of a lot more people in the Bible. Adam's naming of Eve is very significant since it signifies man's divine right to authority, responsibility, acceptance and sense of belonging for the woman that, he is blessed to have in his *life as his wife. [His lost but found rib]*

Everything that God made was good. Every aspect of creation has its significance that goes a long way to teach us with some revelation. The naming of Eve by Adam is no exception. God could have created Eve straight away and named her Himself.

But God gave recognition and respect to Adam. He was given authority and dominion over the earth and all living things as well as the authority to name Eve. This is to teach the woman subordination, an internal and external respect and reverence for man.

The man is to protect and keep the woman in recognition and respect to God for this great responsibility, for it comes with and accountability. The man will account for the love, care, provision, honor and the understanding that he owe to the woman as a command:

1Pet 3:7 "Husbands in the same way be considerate as you live with your wives and treat them with respect as the weaker partner and as heirs with you of the gracious gift of life, so that nothing will hinder your prayers"

CHAPTER THREE

CHARACTERISTICS OF EVE SEEN IN WOMEN CHARACTER STUDY

W e have already studied that Eve was uniquely formed with beauty, glory and honor, in the divine will of God with godly character and righteousness. She was pure and innocent. She was also endowed with abilities and virtues to be Adam's helpmeet.

Likewise every woman is of such virtues until puberty period, perhaps when the consciousness of sin sets in her life especially if one has not had good godly-upbringing or taken care of properly.

The woman is said to be the weaker vessel according to *I Peter 3: 7* she is also more vulnerable to temptation as in:

Gen. 3:6 "so when the woman saw that the tree was good for food, that it was pleasant to the eyes, and a tree desirable to make one wise. She took of its fruit and ate."

*2 Cor. 11:3 "But I fear, lest by any means as the serpent **beguiled** Eve through his **subtlety** so your **minds** should be corrupted from the simplicity that is in Christ."*

Eve exercised her will to disobey God and disrespect her husband.

Disobedient and disrespect are characters very typical of most women.

Eve went near the forbidden fruit, engaged in fruitless and disastrous conversation with Satan.

This was an **unsanctified relationship**.

Like Eve, most women often go to forbidden places only to get themselves involved into serious trouble. Like Eve, some women are fond of keeping wrong relationships.

As a woman, whenever you choose to abandon your protection or covering and get involve in bad company you set yourself up for disaster.

Eve abused her position, privilege and free will: she decided to have her own way to satisfy her unholy desires and definitely did not end her well.

Like Eve, most women sometimes abuse certain positions and honor given them.

Many women in leadership positions try to usurp power and take more advantage of the privileges and limits given to them.

Eve dared to challenge God's authority and chose rather to trust and accept the lies of Satan than depending on God's word.

Women sometimes go all out to satisfy themselves in whatever way possible.

from dubious resources than in the *truth*
...lse prophets and soothsayers)
...nowledge that God gave to Adam and Eve,
...re knowledge above her. She craved for the
...concealed knowledge of the tree of good and

...larly, some women do have some insatiable evil
...re of knowledge. Be careful that your minds are not
corrupted as Eve's check this scripture:

2 Cor. 11:3 "But I fear, lest by any means as the serpent **beguiled Eve** *through his subtlety, so your* **minds** *should be* **corrupted** *from the simplicity that is in Christ."*

Eve beheld the fruit and saw it was good for food, pleasant to the eyes and appealing to appetite.

Gen 3:6 *"and when the woman saw that the fruit was good for food and that it was pleasant to the eyes, and a tree to be desired to make one, wise, she took of the fruit thereof and did eat."*

- *SAW THE FRUIT GOOD FOR FOOD-****Evil appetite***
- *PLEASANT TO THE EYES – **Lust of the eyes***
- *APPEALING TO APPETITE–**Lust of the flesh***
- *ENTICING AMBITION [**Desired to make one wise]** -**Pride of life***

BEWARE NOW OF YOUR STEPS

1st Aspect: Eve 'Saw' the Fruit was 'Good' for Food

It was the *'seeing'* that opened the door to sin. Our eyes are the gateway to our hearts. The eyes affect our hearts with joy, grief, good, evil as well as guilt.

A great deal of sin has come into the hearts of women by our eyes.

YES! We look at *vanity* (vain and evil things). We envy, become jealous, covet and desire good as well as things that may be evil, that do not belong to us. Our original old enemy (Satan) is always around and he throws his fiery darts into our eyes, to poison the mind first and then the heart.

So, let us all in agreement with Job make a *covenant* with our *eyes* to refuse to look at things that may put us in danger of lusting. Not all that glitters is gold.

Not all pleasant, appealing and enticing things are good.

Food for example, is good but not all are good foods. We must be careful about what we eat, when and where. Food can be a powerful tool of temptation and downfall:

a.   *Food* can build or break us.
b.   *Food* can heal or wound us.
c.   *Food* can give life and kill as well.

Many are those who through food have been demonized, attacked, diseased, destroyed, poisoned and even killed. Not all good-looking food is good. After all, man shall not live by bread alone.

2nd Aspect: It was Pleasant to the 'Eyes'

The eyes must be greatly controlled and disciplined. If you go near vanity or evil and choose to have a look, whatever you see may or may not look pleasant. But learn to turn away your eyes from things that may seem pleasant in your eyes, which in reality are vanity.

You should discipline your desire especially towards forbidden things. Upon all the fruits God gave Adam and Eve, it was the forbidden fruit Eve desired. How often do we desire to have what belongs to other people after all the blessings God has given us? And pleasant things that may be deadly in disguise.

3rd Aspect: It was 'Appealing' to Appetite.

Our appetites must be seriously controlled; as well unsatisfied appetite could be dangerous. Appetite could be for food, drink, evil and lustful emotions. The Bible warns against lustful desires.

James 1:13-15 "When tempted, no one should say, "God is tempting me." For God cannot be tempted by evil, nor does He tempt anyone; but each one is tempted when, by his own evil desire, he is dragged away and enticed. Then, after desire has conceived, it gives birth to sin; and sin when it is full grown, gives birth to death."

James 4: 7 "Submit yourself, then, to God. Resist the devil and he will flee from you."

It is this desire that raises our appetites. We must desire for godly things, which are in the Word of God.

4th Aspect: It was Enticing to 'Ambition'

An inordinate desire yielded the evil inducement to make Eve sin. Eve was over ambitious. Evil ambition in anything may not be helpful.

Women like Eve are often betrayed into snares by inordinate desires to have their senses gratified.

See how the desire for unnecessary knowledge under the mistaken notion for wisdom proves hurtful and destructive to the generation of mankind.

Only Jesus is the tree to be desired to make one wise.

(I *Cor. 1:30.*) Let us all by faith feed on the knowledge of Him that we might be wise unto salvation. The tree of knowledge will not be forbidden in heaven.

Women must be circumspect or cautious of the type of friendship they make and who persuades, convince or tempt them into attaining just any type of knowledge, which may be different from the knowledge in the Bible. Do not be over anxious Satan can only tempt but not force you. He can persuade us to cast ourselves down. But Satan cannot cast us down.

Note it is easier to learn that which is bad than to teach that which is good.

Gen 3:6b *"she also gave to her husband with her and he ate"*.

Eve found the fruit pleasant rather than deadly. So she persuaded her husband just as Satan persuaded her to eat. Eve gave the fruit to Adam under the color of kindness. She wouldn't eat such delicious fruit alone.

Unfortunately it was the greatest unkindness she ever did to him. Those that have themselves doing evil are commonly willing to draw on others. What do women feed their husbands with? Is it the forbidden food created by the doctor/ nutritionist, which eventually bring disasters? Is it the poorly prepared food? Do you feed them on hatred, resentment and disrespect?

Women let us feed our husbands with love and the care of God, which is the *"bread of life."*

Women, do not use your position and influence wrongly on men. Do not let others share in your sins. Most women like Eve are never satisfied with position, wealth etc. Let us try to be content with whatever God has given us. Stay in whatever limits we are put or placed.

Be obedient to God, your husband and those in authority. Be content with the salvation of Christ and know that only in Jesus is the fullness of life, knowledge and power.

WEAKNESSES OR EVIL ASPECTS OF WOMEN

The Bible is supposed to be our Christian manual. It is therefore proper that we study some examples of certain evil aspects and weaknesses of Biblical women as compared to our lives today. The woman is weak in nature and components. Our weaknesses cannot be hidden or overlooked *(I Pet. 3:7)*. Our mother Eve exhibited this weakness by allowing Satan to outwit her. There are also many aspects of weaknesses observed in Biblical women.

Four Evil Aspects to be studied:

1. Women who stir up *strife.*
2. Women who are *temptress.* (Who entice men to sin)
3. Women who are *seductive* (adulteress and even beyond sexual immorality)
4. Women who are *prostitutes.*

1. Women who stir up Strife:

Prov. 19:13b "Contentious or quarrelsome wives or women are like a constant dripping".

They are like the mosquito buzzing in the night.

Prov. 21:9 "It is better to dwell in loneliness than to stay with a quarrelsome woman"

We all know it is terrible to put up with such people.

2. Women who are Temptress:

Gen 3:6 Eve tempted Adam to sin.
Job's wife persuaded him to curse God.

Job 2:9 "Are you still holding on to your integrity?
Curse God and die."

In Esther 5:14, *Zeresh (Haman's Wife) advised him to ask*
the King to hang Mordecai on gallows.

Matt. 6:22-23, Herodias' daughter, Salama, demanded
the head of John the Baptist immediately on a platter.

Gen. 27: 6-10,
Rebecca helps one of her sons to take his elder brother's
birthright. [This is partiality and discrimination.]

3. Women who are Seductive:
Adultery, this goes beyond sexual immorality to total
destruction, seduction even today is to lead people astray
from God's presence.
Judges 16:6, we see Delilah and Samson where Delilah
is bent on destroying Samson.

In 1 Kings 21:15, "And It came to pass when, Jezebel heard
that Naboth was stoned, and was dead, that Jezebel said to
Ahab, Arise, take possession of the vineyard of
Naboth the Jezreelite, which he refused to give thee for
money: for Naboth is not alive but dead."

Jezebel focused her royal power to a willful and wicked
advantage. She arranged for the murder of Naboth and seized
his vineyard, which Ahab had coveted. But in the end her
body was torn apart by dogs. She personifies the principle of
reaping what you sow. It also demonstrates power and influence of evil, which never triumph over God's limited time
of chastising.
You see, sometimes a woman's manipulation can outdo
all the powers available to a man. Are you or do you know of

any seductive or evil woman? Intercede for her be a woman of good intentions and concern.

4. Women who were Prostitutes:

> *Jude 1: 7b "As Sodom and Gomorrah, and the cities around them in a similar manner to these, having given themselves over to sexual immortality and gone after strange flesh are set forth as an example suffering the vengeance of eternal fire."*

> *I Kings 3:16 "now two women who were harlots came to the king and stood before him."*

Prostitution is highly degrading to womanhood and causes sexual transmitted diseases (e.g. AIDS). Rahab was a harlot who was later saved. *(Josh 2:1)* Mary Magdalene, a harlot was transformed when she met Jesus.

No matter who you are you can also be transformed when you come to Jesus.

CROWNING QUALITIES OF THE WOMAN

Even though women just as Eve exhibit certain unholy characters, women have been created and endowed with certain crowing qualities. Some Biblical women did exhibit these good values.

There are 5 Qualities:

    I.   Devotional Spirit–Hannah, Esther
    II. Modesty - Rebecca
    III. Liberality/ Generosity - Dorcas

IV. Wisdom/Virtues – Pilate's wife
V. Helps - Priscilla (Rom. 16:3-4)

I. Devotional Spirit.

In Sam. 1:10-11, Hannah prayed for a child. *"And she was
in bitterness of soul and prayed to the Lord and wept in
anguish then she made a vow and said,
O Lord of Hosts if you will indeed look on the affliction of
your maidservant and remember me, and not forget your
maidservant, but will give your maidservant a male child,
then I will give him to the Lord all the days of his life and
no razor shall come upon his head."*

Hannah, a barren middle-aged woman prayed all night in supplication to the Lord for a child.

Hannah saw how necessary and effective it was to pray and devoted her time to the Lord. She entered into a serious committed time of prayer and supplication before the Lord. God fulfilled the desires of her heart.

Esther fasted and prayed for favor in her marriage, grace and ability to deliver her people from bondage. She told Modecai:

*Esther 4:16 "Go gather all the Jews who are
present in Shushan and fast for me neither eat not drink for
three days, night or day. My maids and I will fast likewise
and so I will go to the King, which is against the law
and if I perish, I perish."*

Queen Esther in total commitment to sacrifice for her people, decided to devote her time in fasting and prayer in faith coupled with concern.

She recognized the call and urgency on her life, to save her people. She relied on God and chose to pray and it did work.

How prayerful or devoted are you? How sacrificial and concerned are you towards God, your family, church and the nation at large?

II. Modesty

In Gen. 24:65 "for she had said to the servant 'who is this man walking in the field to meet us' the servant said 'it is my master,' so she took a veil and covered herself with it."

Unveiling of a woman comes after the marriage as a token of humility, modesty and subjection.

(Another precious virtue)

New relationship requires a lot of careful attitudes.

Rebecca was a virgin, modest, chaste and humble. Those that by faith are espoused to Christ and would be presented, as chaste virgins to Him must be in conformity to His example, humble themselves like Rebecca, who alighted from the horse, when she saw her husband, Isaac on foot.

It would be of great respect and honor for young women who are not yet married to exercise patience, cover themselves up till their wedding day. (***Virginity preserved***)

I Timothy 2:9; "In like manner also that the women adorn themselves in modest apparel with prosperity and modera-tion, not with braided hair or gold or pearls or costly clothing, but which is proper for women professing godli-ness with good works."

I Peter 3:2b, "Women with disobedient, unbelieving husband can win them by being chaste, modest coupled by the fear of God."

May God in His goodness and merciful kindness grant women these virtues.

III. Liberality/Generosity

Giving; in *Luke 8:2-3*, Mary Magdalene, of whom seven demons were cast out and Joanna the wife of Chuza, Herod's steward and Susanna, and many others, all provided for Jesus from their substance. Many women gave to support Jesus' ministry.

Luke 2:14 "For all these out of their abundance have put offerings for God, but she out of her poverty put in all the livelihood that she had".

The widow is supposed to be the poorest in the society but she gave her all, wholeheartedly and liberally.

John 12:3, the anointing of Jesus, feet by Mary Magdalene with expensive oil was to show honor and humility. She gave out all that she had and was rewarded. A form of worship.

Are you generous? Are you caring, do you have a giving spirit? Sarah also did kindness to an angel unknowingly and was greatly blessed (*Gen. 18: 1-8*). All who give cheerfully or liberally were rewarded. There is more blessing in giving than receiving. Learn to be liberal.

IV. Wisdom/Virtues:

Prov. 12:4; "excellent wife is the crown of her husband, but one who causes shame is like rotten bone"

Prov. 14:1. "Wise women build, keep or maintain their house and make it thrive. The foolish once pulls down her possession and relationship and destroys her own effort."

Prov. 11:16 "gracious woman retains honor with quiet victories of beautiful character."

Prov. 31:30 "above all beauty and charm are deceit but the woman who fears the Lord shall be praised–she is wise."

Pilate's wife gave good and wise counsel to her husband pertaining to the death of Christ. What kind of counsel do you give to your husband? Whatever position or capacity you find yourself, do your best to give godly or god-fearing counsel.

BIBLICAL RIGHTS OF WOMEN

Woman is created for great works and responsibilities. She has numerous duties, but her biblical rights are also spelt out. This session teaches *biblical rights and authority* of the woman.

Gen. 2:24 spells out a wife's right and bond to her husband in marriage, the matrimonial home and life in general. Together with Adam, Eve was to co-rule the earth.

Prov 31:27 a woman's right over running and managing the affairs of the household. A woman should exercise her right well.

Prov 23:13-14, the right and authority to discipline children without any interference. How well do you discipline your children?

I Cor. 7:4; her right over her Husband's body. It is not the husband alone who should exercise his right and authority over the wife's body.

Num 27:8 the inheritance rights; Women or daughters can inherit the father's possession, likewise her husband's.

Judges, 13:22-23; Right to counsel her husband. (Pilate's wife gave wise counsel to her husband.)

Dan. 5:10, Belshazzar's mother the queen gave wise counsel and encouragement to his son the king about Daniel.

How, when and what kind of counsel do you offer your husband, children and as leaders?

*Deut 24:17 ''Thou shall not pervert the judgment
neither of the stranger, nor of the fatherless nor take a
widow's raiment to pledge''.
Widows must be cared for and protected.*

Women deserve the right to transparency from husband
and children and [vise versa] in every aspect especially in
monetary matters. Things concealed or kept secret from each
other cripples the trust in the home.

CHAPTER FOUR

THE FALL OF OUR FIRST PARENTS

The story about the fall of Adam and Eve is a sad one. We have learnt of the pleasant view of the holiness and happiness of our first parents in the Garden of Eden, with the grace and favor of God, the peace and beauty of whole creation. Indeed everything was very good. The scene however, was altered with the account of sin and misery of our first parents.

The wrath and curse of God was against them. The peace and harmony of creation was distorted, its beauty soiled and stained. How has the gold become dim and most fine gold changed, what has become of paradise, a place of holiness, delight and pleasure, with all its blessings? Oh! How our hearts be affected with these records!

This story is very important and a concern for all mankind. For by one man sin entered the world and death by sin and so death passed unto all men:

For that all men have sinned; this account will be in five 5 parts. The 5th has great impact on our lives today.

In this temptation, first God gave them prohibition or command *Gen 3:1-5*. We analyze these as follows:

Part 1- Gen 3:1-5
Who tempted Eve?
How and what was Eve tempted to do?
With what was she tempted?
Why this temptation at all?

Part 2 - Gen 3:6-8

The tempted Eve, her defeat and transgression:
What moved Eve to sin?
What are the steps of transgression?
The ultimate consequences of transgression.

Part 3- Gen 3:9-15

The transgressors were arraigned before the righteous God.
Our first parents were rebuked after they confessed their sin. Their crime was seen in their confession.

Part 4 - Gen 3:14-19
The tempter-Satan the chief agent, (*vs. 14-15*)
The tempted-woman or Eve, an innocent victim.
The man-Adam yielding to his wife (*vs. 17-19*)

Part 5: *Gen 2:16-17*
Consider the significance of this account and its impact on mankind till today. Adam and Eve disobeyed the command God gave hence the transgression and subsequent judgments.

The Temptation of Eve: Part one
Gen. 3:1-5

Satan in the likeness of a serpent chose to disguise himself as a cunning or shrewd creature, clever than any other beast of the field.

Satan lured Eve into sin by engaging in a conversation with her with questions about God's instructions or command about the forbidden fruit.

The serpent contradicted God's command.

Thus is the **subtlety of Satan**.

The serpent that was used to blemish the reputation of divine law, enticed Eve to sin.

Eve was tempted to **eat of the forbidden fruit of the tree of knowledge of good and evil.**

Why this temptation at all or why did Satan do this?

Satan was a malignant spirit. By creation he was an angel of light and an immediate attendant before God's throne. But sin made Satan to become an apostate from his first state and a rebel against God's crown and dignity. As a ringleader and prince of the devils, he *was enraged against God and His glory.* Satan became *envious of man and his happiness.*

His aim was to draw our first parents and *mankind to sin and so brought separation between them and their God.*

Satan or devil from beginning of creation was a murderer and a great mischief-maker. Satan is still fighting against the children of God to destroy and separate them from God. *He is trying to stop us from inheriting eternity as heirs of the heavenly throne.*

Adam and Eve before the falls lived right with God, and were enjoying a wonderful relationship with God until Satan succeeded in getting Eve to sin and hence ushered in sin and death into the world.

The Tempted Eve, Defeat and Transgression Part 2
Gen 3: 6-8

Eve exercised her will to obey Satan rather than to fear God's command. It was the *inducement* (evil desire for the fruit) that made Eve to sin. The tempter's clever management of lies deceived her. God permitted it for the fulfillment of prophecy.

The steps to Transgression

To begin with Eve should not have gone near the forbidden fruit at all.

She should not have *entertained* Satan by *entering* into a *conversation* with him.

More so, she should have *turned away* her *eyes* from beholding *vanity*; but she entered into *temptation* by *looking* with *pleasure* on the *forbidden* fruit. The fruit was appealing to appetite and Eve had an *evil appetite* (lust). It was also *enticing* to *ambition* she also *coveted* to be *wise* above what was given her.

Eve's decision to eat the fruit is equal to stealing since neither God nor her husband gave her the permission or instructed her to taste of it. One step of sin leads to another. The sin of *disobedience* led Eve to the *lust of the eyes, appetite, ambition that is the pride of life.*

Adam could not rebuke his wife but rather fell into sin himself. He who is the head with all the authority could not stop Satan.

He *obeyed his wife rather* than God's command. Adam sinned against knowledge and honor. He sinned against light, love and peace in the Garden of Eden.

Check this; when Eve ate nothing happened:

*Gen 3:6b-7 "And gave also unto her husband and he did eat. And **the eyes of them both were opened, and they knew they were naked....**"*

But the scriptures record the effect and results of eating of the fruit-Adam [man] who was the foundation of the earth met his downfall together with his wife affecting the life of the whole universe.

When the devil succeeds in destroying the man of the home he automatically destroys the whole family. Satan is surely attacking men; fathers, husband leaders both great and small and even ministers of the gospel. Watch out men!

The Ultimate Consequences of Sin: Gen. 3:7

"Then the eyes of them both were opened and they knew that they were naked; and the sewed fig leaves together and made themselves aprons".

Thus was the experimental knowledge of good and evil. The eyes of their conscience were opened, and their hearts smote them for what they had done.

Shame and guilt overwhelmed them. They knew they were naked and sewed fig leaves together to make themselves coverings. They were stripped, deprived of all the honor and joy of their paradise estate. They were exposed to all miseries that may be expected from an angry God. They were disarmed, their defense taken away and ashamed forever before God and His angels. They were naked indeed because they were disrobed of all their ornaments and ensigns of honor, degraded from their dignity, and disgraced in the highest degree.

They were laid open to the contempt and reproach of heaven and their own conscience. Their eyes, as wished by Satan, were opened **but** to **shame** and **grief** not to their honor and advantage as promised by Satan. (**Gen. 3:4-5**)

Fear also seized them after eating of the forbidden fruit. They feared God's presence.

Vs. 8 *"and they heard the sound of the Lord God walking in the garden in the cool of the day and Adam and his wife hid themselves from the presence of the Lord God among the trees of the garden."*

God came as a judge His approach frightened them. His still, small voice that was heard at a distance sounded the notice of His coming. Before they sinned, the sound of God's coming to them meant a loving visit of which they would have run to meet Him and with a humble joy welcomed His gracious visit.

However, owing to sin and subsequent shame, it had become otherwise. God had become a **terror** to them and they were confused. Their own conscience accused them and set their sin before them in its proper colors. God had come against them like **enemies**.

The fig leaves could not help them. The **whole earth** was at **war with them with no mediator between them** and God. There was nothing remained but a fearful God looking for judgment. It was in this *fright* that they hid themselves among bushes. They fled for the same mistake, knowing they were **guilty**; they could not stand a trial but absconded and fled from justice. That was the consequence of transgression.

With the falsehood and fallacies of Satan the tempter, our first parents lost fellowship with God. Man is still in sin of disobedience, which is the **key sin**. So shame, fear, grief, terror and confusion keep attacking us.

Part 3 - The Transgressors Arraigned and Put before the Righteous God. Gen 3:9-13

Adam and Eve were caught and put before God the righteous judge. Adam was called to stand a trial before God with the question *"where art thou?"* The question sounded as if God did not know where Adam was but it was to create an awareness of their crime and rebuke them to confess themselves.

He called Adam and not Eve since Adam was expected to have known better and to have shown more maturity and responsibility than Eve. Adam responded to His call in fear by confessing his guilt.

*Gen 3:10-13 "And he said, I heard thy voice in the garden and I was afraid, because I was **naked** and I hid myself. And He said, who told thee that thou wast naked? Hast thou eaten of the tree, whereof I commanded thee that thou shouldest not eat?*
*And the man said, the woman whom thou gavest to be with me **she gave me**, of the **tree**, and I **did** eat.*
*And the Lord God said unto the woman, what is this that thou has done? And the **woman** said the **serpent beguiled me** and I **did eat**."*

This meant Adam had realized his fault, shame and guilt. They confessed of fear and nakedness by this, God who knew the outcome of eating the forbidden fruit knew they had disobeyed Him. Adam we see tries to shift the blame on Eve instead of accepting his failure to exercise his authority and obedience to God (rather than yielding to his wife 's persuasion).

Eve blamed the serpent instead of accepting her disobedience to God's command.

Men today must learn to be more *responsible* and obedient to God's word, and women must learn to be *obedient* and submissive be *content* with whatever has been made *available* to them each person must accept his or her failures and repent rather than *apportioning blames*.

Part 4- The Sentence Passed on Them: Gen 3:14-15

The curse pronounced on Satan:
Satan was already convicted of rebellion against God. His malice and wickedness was so notorious and could not be found by any secret search.

Satan was to be forever excluded from all hope of pardon because he had no thought for repentance.

The sentence passed upon the 'tempter' might be considered as too light upon the serpent, a brute creature which Satan made use of. Therefore to testify displeasure against sin and a jealousy for the injured honor, which God conferred upon Adam and Eve, God put a curse and reproach upon the serpent, and is now burdened:

Romans. 8:20 "for the creature was made subject of vanity, not willingly but by reason of him who (Satan) hath subjected the same in no hope."

Satan was the first to sin so he was first to be judged. God hates sin, and is especially displeased with those who entice others into sin.

God cursed Satan and said:

Gen 3:14 "Because thou hast done this,
thou art cursed above all cattle and more than every beast
of the field. On your belly shall thou go,
ye shall eat dust all days of your life."

Understand the mystery of curse. For instance, subtle tempters are the most accursed creatures under the sun. Subtlety often proves a great curse to man. The serpent is here made man's reproach and enmity. He is to be forever looked upon as vile and despicable creature and a proper object of scorn and contempt. *'Upon thy belly'* meaning no longer upon his feet or half erect, but by crawling with its belly cleaving to the earth.

This is an expression of a very abject and miserable condition. When we are also disobedient to God and sin we find ourselves in a similar condition.

Psalm 44:25 "For our soul is bowed down to the dust: our belly cleaveth unto the earth"

His crime was he tempted Eve to eat that which she **should not**. His punishment was he was necessitated to eat that which he **would not**. *'Dust shall thou eat'* denotes not only a base and despicable condition, but also a mean and pitiful spirit.

It is said that those whose courage has departed from them are the people that lick the 'dust like a serpent' *(Micah. 7:17)*.

Satan was to be forever looked upon as a venomous, noxious creature and a proper object of hatred and destitution.

The Curse continues:

Gen 3:15 "I will put an enmity between thee and the woman; between thy seed and her seed."

The serpent is now cursed and the only creature who must turn against man and man against it.

Gen 49: 17 "He (the seed of the woman) shall crush your (Satan) head and you shall bruise his heels."

The serpent is indeed hurtful to man and often bruises man's heels. But man is victorious over the serpent (Satan) when Jesus Christ bruised his head through the work on cavalry cross. Jesus' mortal wounds on the cross were aimed at destroying the whole nature of vipers.

Satan is subtle and very dangerous. Yet he could not prevail in the destruction of mankind. This pronouncement is fortified by:

Psalm 91:13 "thou shall thread upon the lion and adder."

Mark 16:18 'they shall take up serpents...'

This is good promise from God to His people.

The serpent and the woman were friendly and familiar behind closed doors concerning the forbidden fruit with a wonderful agreement between them.

But now they are irreconcilably set at variance. Sinful friendship would by all means end up in mortal feud. Those that unite in wickedness will not unite long. This sentence may be considered as leveled against the devil that used the serpent as his vehicle in those appearances, while he was the principal agent.

He that spoke through the serpent's side and was principally intended in the sentence was like the pillar of cloud and fire. He has a dark side towards the devil and a bright side towards our first parents and their seeds.

The record of *Gen. 3:15* can also be called the 1st prophecy of the coming of the Messiah, which is known in Latin literally, as *"proteveluim"* This is also known as the 1st *preaching of the gospel.*

The word *"seed"* in the Old Testament is used to refer to offspring and descendants in general. The woman is of great importance because she was the 'mother of the living' and through her the savior would come. The seed came to the woman by the Holy Spirit over shadowing her (the virgin birth).

This messianic interpretation is justified since the crushing of the serpent's head implies a mortal wound. On the other hand, the bruising of the heel is not too fatal. This was a reference made to the savior's suffering and it was only a preparation for his victorious resurrection.

The Judgment on Eve

The judgment passed on Eve was more of chastisement to bring repentance to Eve rather than a curse to bring ruin. God did not use the word *'curse'* as in Satan's case.

Gen. 3:16 God said: "I will increase your trouble in pregnancy and your desire and your pain in giving birth. And your desire will be for your own husband, yet you will be subject to him."

There are 2 Aspects of Condemnation:
A state of sorrow
A state of subjection

A. A State of Sorrow

1. Multiplication of grief or suffering in conception and childbirth. Childbirth, which is supposed to be a blessing to the woman, was now distorted by the phrase.

Gen 3:16 "your sorrow in conception will be greatly multiplied."

This is due to sin, some stress includes:
In conception and childbirth women receive or undergo impressions of grief, frustration, fear, anxiety within the mind and emotions.

The travailing throes (agonizing pain) and in disposition before, trials of nursing of a child and the vexation after. Women are liable to common calamities e.g. sickness, miscarriage etc. What is more if the child proves wicked, foolish and stubborn? Such a child is more than ever the heaviness compounded on the mother that bore him. Showers of blessing, blessing of the womb.

Psalm 127:3 "Lo children are a heritage [blessing]....", children are good gifts from God, and they are His blessing. But many become showers of pain and *multiple sorrows.* Every pain and every groan of the travailing woman speaks aloud the consequences of sin.

But in all these pains and agonies God's loving care is always available to see us through, for the joy and pride of having a baby. He also cares when mothers pray, their prayers are very effective and God honors 'the *mother's prayer'* so *mothers do not stop praying for your children.*

B. State of Subjection

Gen. 3:16b "Your desire shall be for your husband and he shall rule over you"

1) Your desires or craving will be for your husband, be it in sexual or psychological desires. The same Hebrew word "teshuquah" meaning turn towards is the root word for crave.
2) He shall rule over you, in Hebrew, rule *is 'marshal,' 'rule-ship' or ' mastery.'*
3) Every woman who is normal [human-being] desires / craves for a man. It is natural and normal.
4) But your desire must be well disciplined in the way of the Lord.

88

For centuries this has been used as a yardstick against women either to totally subjugate them or severely restrict their talents. Adam and Eve who were equal in authority and responsibility at creation are now different.

Remember, the more you desire the more you would be 'ruled over.' So get prepared! The woman is now powerless. She cannot assume authority in:

I Timothy 2:11-12 "A woman should learn in quietness and full submission."

The woman is now under the dominion of her husband. She is no more at her own disposal but to surrender,

become docile to the subjection of the husband. The reason: Adam was first created and not Eve.

Adam was not deceived but Eve. She fell first and was the means of seducing the husband.

Eve was given to be a helper but proved to be a most grievous hindrance, even the instrument of Adam's fall and ruin. On this the bond of subjection was confirmed and tied on her. Christ is the head and Savior of the church. God will have a resemblance of Christ's authority over the church as the husband's authority over the wife. Just as Christ is the head of the church to protect and save it, to supply it with all good things and secure and deliver her from evil.

So is the husband's authority over the wife to keep her from injuries and to provide comfortably for her according to his ability.

The woman is to submit in harmony and obedience.

Submit in compliance to God's command and authority, God's honor and leadership. The woman should not assume or take with force the position of a man.

The woman is to have a mind suited to her rank and not to covet very higher places or positions more than she deserve.

Eph. 5:21-23; "Submit yourselves to one another because of your reverence to Christ's."

Vs. 22 "wives submit to your own husbands as to the Lord. For a husband has authority over his wife just as Christ has authority over the church; and Christ is himself the savior of the church His body."

All Christians owe mutual submissiveness to one another. We need to be of yielding and submissive spirit. In mutual submission, all related duties in the church and the nation would be better performed. If Eve had not sinned, women would obey in love, humility and meekness and Adam's dominion would have been no grievance at all.

Therefore women ought not to complain of just and godly subjection from their husbands and authority even when it appears harsh. However women should stay away from sin and disobedience and make committed effort to obey the Word and submit in the love as unto the Lord.

THE 3 DEADLY 'Ds'

Women, who try to **disobey, despise and dominate** their husbands, violate divine law, thwart divine order or command, which brings untold hardship on them, and sorrow to the family and the nation at large.

Upon all these there is **goodness**, God's wrath is mixed with mercy and compassion. For instance, there is sorrow in childbirth after which is the *joy* that a new child is born alive, healthy and well. John 16:21:

"A woman when she is in travail had sorrow, because her hour is come but as soon as is delivered of the child, she remembereth no more the anguish, for Joy that a man is born into the world."

Subjection to your own husband should not be seen as punishment but love and humility in obedience as unto the Lord. The woman is subject to her husband only not to a stranger or an enemy. But humble to authority in all aspects of life

The Judgment on Adam

Adam was condemned for heeding to his wife instead of God's command. His excuse for shifting blame to his wife was rejected by God. Eve sinned by persuasion from Satan but Adam sinned deliberately. God will likewise refuse frivolous excuses on judgment day.

There are 3 Marks of Displeasure

1st Mark of Displeasure

Gen. 3: 17,
"Curse is the ground for thy sake in sorrow shall thou eat all the days of your life"

The comfort, joy, honors of distinguished and blessed paradise is now a cursed, dishonored, miserable and barren habitation for man. Its productions are now weeds and briers subjecting the property on it to vanity.

The curse of the earth has cut off all expectation of happiness in things below. Man must now be quickened to look for bliss and satisfaction in things from above.

2ND Mark of Displeasure

Verse 19 "In sweat of your face you shall eat bread, till you return to the ground".

91

Before the curse Adam had all the pleasure of the garden to himself and the garden well dressed without extra effort by him. Now he shall look for meat, waste his strength and afflict his mind. The curse also speaks of the difficulties, which through the infirmity of the flesh would require man's labor in the service of God. The earth, **which was man's home, has been cursed.** Now that man's home has been cursed against him, how can man have life easy? But blessed be to our Lord and Savoir Jesus Christ that our labor will not be in vain. Man's food now is bitterness of the soul instead of God's divine favor, which is *life* and *the bread of life.*

3ʳᵈ *Mark of Displeasure*

Vs. 19b "Thou art dust and into dust shall thou return"

Adam was reminded of the origin and meaning of his name. *(Red earth)* Death has been declared and established as consequences or wages of sin and as definite inevitable end of man. The grant of immortality was thus withdrawn together with the power and the breath of life put forth in him from the beginning of creation.

The spirit and the soul of man, which stand for God's breath of life in man shall forsake him (man) making him a lump of dust. Beloved in Christ, our strength is not like stones, but light and weak like dust.

A great man is just a great mass of dust (without the breath, wisdom, power, knowledge and the fear of God) and will definitely return into dust.

Heb 9: 27 states: "it is appointed unto man once to die and after that the judgment."

This reminds us of the accountability that awaits us after death.

Ecclesiastes 3:2 *"There is a time to be born and a time to die"*

This also reminds us not to forget death; for once we are born we shall surely die. It will be of immense help and blessing for us if we realize this mystery of life, fear God and His word, obey Him and live right so as to inherit the kingdom of God and have access to our original glory, honor and happiness in the Lord. We must endeavor to fit ourselves appropriately into God's plan for our lives.

The Expulsion from the Garden of Eden

The sin of disobedience, greed, evil desire and ambition has really caught up with the original couple. God's love, care and protection have been changed to wrath.

This automatically led to the expulsion of our first parents.

Gen. 3:22-24 "The lord God said,
Behold, the man has become like one of us, to know good and evil. And now, lest he put out his hand and takes also of the tree of life and eats and live forever –
therefore the Lord sent him out of the garden of Eden to till the ground from which he was taken."

Adam was expelled from the gracious Garden of Eden. This was to awaken and humble them to bring them to their sense of sin and folly. It is also to bring them unto repentance. God sent Adam out even though he was not willing to leave. This signifies the exclusion of him from all the bliss and the glory of paradise.

Communication and acquaintance was broken off. Adam's expulsion meant he was unworthy of the honor and incapable of God's services. So Adam and all mankind by the fall forfeited and lost communication with the good creator. Man was sent out of the garden to toil the ground. His tilling the ground would be recompensed or rewarded by his eating of its fruit, keep him humble and sober and to remind him of his latter end.

However, upon all what Adam and Eve had done, God did not abandon them to despair. God sent his Cherubim with the flaming sword to protect the garden wherein was the tree of life so that Adam could neither steal nor force an entry.

But it was henceforth in vain for him to expect righteousness, life and happiness.

God did not drive Adam away in despair, but to assist him look for real life and the happiness in the "promised seed", by which the flaming sword would be removed. Hence the way unto the Holies was consecrated and laid down for us.

God's Care for Adam and Eve after the Fall.

God's care for Adam and Eve after sinning was: He corrects His disobedient children; put them under marks of displeasure. Yet God did not disinherit them.

God provided the herbs of the field for food and coats of skin for their clothing. God Jehovah Jireh still provides for us all and we have no needs.

Gen. 3:21 "Unto Adam also and to his wife did the Lord God made coats of skins and clothed them."

If it pleased God to kill them, he would have left them naked and shameful.

Sin made them naked to their shame.

Clothes came in with sin. Adam and Eve became aware of their nakedness and went in pursuit of clothes (fig leaves) to cover up. God made their clothes warm, strong and very plain. Folks should be content having food and covering without complaining.

The rich should not make the wearing of expensive clothes his worship and adoration but that which acknowledges God for who He is and for is divine provision.

The coats of skins given them were from slain beasts. This is to testify the great sacrifice of our Lord and Savior Jesus Christ. The skins given to man for clothing signifies that, Jesus offered His suffering to God as sweet smelling savor and we are to cloth ourselves with His righteousness.

Eve's apron of fig tree was too narrow to cover her up; but God's coats of skin were large, strong, and durable fit for her. Such is the righteousness of Christ. Therefore let us endeavor to put on Jesus Christ. That is, His life, principles, manner and love such as God's care for Adam and Eve. God still cares for us, even while we were yet sinners,

Christ died for us. After all our evil deeds, the love, mercy, and compassion of God never cease great is His faithfulness, morning-by-morning new mercies we see.

The warmth of God's love and protection is always available. Both men and woman should not sin because the grace of God abounds but they should strive to live in holiness.

CHAPTER FIVE

THE VIRTUOUS WOMAN

STEPS TO BE A VIRTUOUS WOMAN

Beloved, a lot has been studied about Eve, our first mother as comparison to our lives as women. For the chapters ahead we shall be searching through the steps to be a virtuous woman, as spoken of in:

Prov.31: 10 "a virtuous woman who can find?
For her price is far above rubies."

We learnt in Gen. 2 of the peace, splendor and the harmony of Adam and Eve in the Garden of Eden. We also learnt of the sin of disobedience, which called for the anger of God, judgment and subsequent curse on them. The judgment on Adam and Eve and the curse on Satan were so grievous and incompatible. [Inseparable]

"And I will put enmity between you and the woman and between your seed and her seed. He shall crush your head and you shall bruise his heel."

Enmity was not between Eve and Satan alone, but between her seed and his (Satan) seed. Satan is therefore at war with women every minute and second of our lives. Most often than not he (Satan) succeeds in destroying us especially if we do not know Christ or have not accepted and surrendered our lives in totality to God.

Friend in Christ for this reason it is fit and proper, in fact very necessary that every woman who wants to be virtuous turn to our Lord and Savior Jesus. Woman you must saved.

Ps. 51:5 'we are all conceived and born in Sin'.
Rom. 3:10 "for there is no one righteous no not one".
Rom. 3:23 "for all have sinned and come short of the glory of God."
John 3:3 "unless a man is born again, he cannot enter the Kingdom of God."
Rom. 10:14 "for whomsoever calls on the name of the Lord shall be saved"
1 John 4:15, "whoever confess that Jesus Christ is the Son of God, God abides in him."

You need to know Christ and know Him better.

Surrender in totality to Him confess and call on Him and you are assured of divine salvation. You need to crave and yearn for the new life in Christ; the old carnal life should be done away with.

The virtuous woman, whose price is far above rubies, need to realize the need for a change; a change from the old sinful life to a new righteous life.

Before a woman can be called virtuous, or excellent than all, she needs to be pure and holy because no filthy and

unholy thing can be called precious, let alone *"more precious than gold"*. Know that we have already been cleansed and purged by the precious Blood of Jesus.
(I Peter 1:18-19)

I Peter 2:4; 'we are like Christ, a precious living stone'. We are indeed children of God. Read Rom. 8:14-17

We can only claim the son-ship of God by knowing and being committed to the following aspects of salvation:

REPENTANCE: *Change of mind*; don't forget you were born in sin. Get godly sorrow for your sin and the *desire to come out of it.*

Rev. 2:5 "Remember where you have fallen and repent."

BE REGENERATED: *Change in nature.*
(An impartation of the Holy Spirit)

Rom. 8: 14 "for as many as are led by the spirit of God, they are the Son of God."

John 3:5-7 "Jesus answered, Very, very I say unto thee except a man be born of water and the Spirit, he cannot enter the kingdom of God.

Vs. 6 that which is born of the flesh is flesh, and which is born of the Spirit is spirit. Marvel not that I said unto thee, ye must be born again."

Your corrupt and evil nature must change:

SANCTIFICATION: *Change in character and conduct*
(Set apart-Holy)

> *2 Cor. 5:17 "if a person be in Christ,*
> *he is a new creation."*

> *1Pet.1: 16 "be holy for 1 am holy."*

JUSTICATION: *Change in standing*; formerly condemned of sin. But now God acquits a sinner and declares him righteous:

> *Roman 8:1-2 "there is therefore now no condemnation of those who are in Christ Jesus."*

ADOPTION: *Change in position;* formerly in the devil's domain but now accepted and adopted by Christ as heirs to the heavenly throne.

> *Gal. 3:29 "and if you are in Christ then you are Abraham's seed and heirs according to the promise."*

Crave for the salvation of Christ and be an heir to the throne.

A woman of excellence can never be without the basic salvation message. You need faith and boldness to decide for a new change in your life. This will give you the fear of God and that is the beginning of wisdom, without wisdom you cannot excel.

> *Prov. 31:31 "charm and beauty is deceit, but the woman who fears God will be praised."*

Change from the old self to a new self of God's wisdom and be filled with His spirit.

The woman wanting to be virtuous needs to go through the steps of salvation; the process of being saved, that is repentance, regeneration, sanctification, justification and adoption and be baptize in water.

A virtuous woman must have Holy Ghost baptism, which is the seal and the power for service to God and man. She must be a spirit- filled woman because we have no power of our own. A Christian depends on the Holy Spirit without Him we can do nothing.

How can one become a Spirit- filled woman?

One needs to be spiritually disciplined.

Spiritual discipline means to desire and crave for the things of God. Always full of cheerful life to share these are the fruits of the Spirit:

Gal 5:22; Love, joy, peace, longsuffering, gentleness, faith and good temperance.

Spiritual discipline means to be **wise and fear** God. Charm and beauty of a woman is nothing compared **to the fear of God**. *[Prov. 31:30]*

Phil. 2:12b, 13 ''Work out your own salvation with fear and trembling. For it God which worketh in you to and to do His good pleasure.''

The fear of God implies obedience, submission and right living with God.

Ps. 111:10; the fear of God, is the beginning of **wisdom**.
Job. 28:28; the fear of God *is* wisdom.
Proverbs. 1:7, 9:10 the fear of God is the beginning of **knowledge**.
Proverbs 8:13; the fear of God is to **hate evil.**
Proverbs 10:27; the fear of God **prolongs** days.

Proverbs. 22:4; the fear of God brings **riches and honor.**

Divine **Spirit of Grace** [*favor*] is that which brings spiritual beauty to a woman, making her that woman of virtue.

The **key secret** to being a virtuous woman is the **fear of God**, which brings upon your life the abundant blessings and God's favor. You are wise when you walk in this fear of God. A foolish woman does not fear God and can never be called virtuous. A woman who is spiritually filled is spiritually disciplined. She is god-fearing therefore she is wise, intelligent, righteous and blessed.

Romans 8:14 "For as many as are led by the **Spirit of God** *these are the sons of God."*

Another quality of a spirit-filled, god-fearing, and disciplined woman who desires to be virtuous is the need to have an effective and acceptable lifestyle with a total commitment, delighting in the things of God.

You should: Set your **priorities** right:

Make Jesus and His kingdom the first thing in your life.

Let God direct you in every decision- making, so you can get the **perfect will** of God.

Luke 12:31 "Seek ye first the kingdom of God and its righteousness and all other things shall be added unto you."

Make His service your delight and He will make your wants His care.

Engage in effective and acceptable lifestyle of **prayer and fasting** study

Isaiah 58:3-14; this is the type fasting that looses the bands of wickedness breaking of yokes and setting the oppressed free, caring and forgiving people.

Pray with the right motive not selfish prayers:

James 4:3 "You ask and do not receive, because you ask a miss that you may spend it on your own pleasures."

Have a *forgiving spirit.* Forgive and ye shall be forgiven do not harbor or nurture bitterness.

Be conscious of the price Jesus paid for you and be prepared to sacrifice for Him, forsaking everything and everybody for His sake.

Love the word, study the word lean on the **word**, live by the **word** walk with the **word**, work and feed on the **word** and so prosper with the **word**. Yes! **The Word** is our Lord and Savior Jesus Christ:

John 1:1-4 "in the beginning was the word..."
Psalm 119:105 " Your word is a lamp unto my feet and a light unto my path."

The woman claiming to be virtuous carries positive value system. She is an exemplary to others in all things be it spiritual, mental, physical, social and financial endeavors.

EXPOSITORY OF PROVERBS 31:10-31

"The virtuous woman who can find, for her price is far above rubies." Proverbs 31:1-3

This verse gives a picture of who gave these words of prophecy to king Lemuel who is interpreted to be king Solomon.

This poem was believed to have been written by Solomon, the chapter starts with:

*"The words of King Lemuel the prophecy that his mother
Beth Sheba taught him. What my son? And what the son of
my womb? And the son of my vows? Give not thy ways unto
women or thy ways to that which destroys kings."*

Exaltation to Lemuel a young prince to take heed of the
sins he would be tempted to and to do the duties of the place
he was called to. It was a prohibition against illicit relationship with women. Lemuel was to look for a woman with
noble character to marry who will demonstrate the principles of wisdom of the home. Many interpreters are of the
opinion Lemuel is Solomon, the mother gave him that name
which signifies one that is of God [Jedediah] 'beloved of the
Lord.'

It is good therefore that mothers teach their children
what is good that they may do it and what is evil that they
may avoid.

Who is this Woman?
What does she stand for? Our next focus is on the

The Biblical Virtuous woman and then the practical life of women:
What qualified her for such high acclamation?
What is the secret behind her virtuous values?
The phrase *"who can find?"*
Gives an introductory tone to the subject meaning.

All women should strive to be *virtuous*. Such women are
very scarce to find and it is this type of a woman that a man
should seek to marry. *I Peter 3:7* states that a woman is the
weaker vessel, but she is made strong by wisdom, grace and
the fear of God:

*Proverbs 31:30b "the woman who fears the Lord, shall
be praised." (Lifted).*

There can be many wives, but it is worthwhile to find a virtuous one even though it may not be easy. The name of this woman was not mentioned. The description of her was made. She stands for high quality virtues.

The biblical version of this woman and what made her qualify to attain such acclamation is detailed in:

Prov. 31:11- 28.
This woman is no particular person but all women who strive to achieve such excellence.

A virtuous woman is a woman of a good spirit.

She has command of her own spirit and knows how to manage other people.

She is pious (holy), industrious and a perfect helpmate for a man.

She teaches good and godly principles and, is firm and steady to them.

She is not frightened with winds and clouds from any part of her duty.

Vs. 10b, "her price is far above rubies"

Denotes that both men and women put value on precious ornaments and attaches great importance to them.

The price of a virtuous woman is far above all the riches or precious ornaments with which women adorn themselves. Such good wives are a blessing and valued. The Bible's qualifications of the virtuous woman in *Prov.31: 11-31:*

In Vs. 11 "the heart of her husband doth safely trust in her, so that he shall have no need of spoil."

The purpose of the creation of the woman was to be a man's *"helpmeet."* So her first responsibility is towards the husband. The first virtue of the woman is *"Trust"* from her husband. Other words used in this verse are constantly, relies, believes and safely. All these words denote complete unity between the husband and the wife. They are united together in spirit, soul and body.

Indeed they have agreement for their purpose in life. He trusts in her conduct to speak in all companies and discretion. She is prudent and uses discretion at all times, so as not to cause the man either damage or reproach. Her chastity is trusted. She never gives her husband the least impression to suspect her or be jealous over her.

She can definitely be relied on. He trusts in her fidelity to his interest that she will never betray his counsels nor have any interest separate from that of his family.

The heart of this woman's husband is at peace. She honors his initiatives at all times. She respects her husband's views. She is content with their lives be it more or less. She is not forceful or demanding i.e. *"she does not push him husband to the wall."*

She is not morose and reserved, but modest and brave. Her countenance has all the marks of virtue, her husband is aware of it and so his heart doth safely believe and confides in her.

He trusts and confides in her.

Her husband is happy and does not envy others who have so much of the wealth of the world. He finds his wife enough for him.

She contributes so much to his content and satisfaction that, he is not a prey for others.

She makes her constant business to do him good.

She is indeed a trustworthy woman as the husband is also good to her.

> *Vs. 12 "She will do him good and not evil*
> *all the days of her life".*

She comforts, encourages and does a lot of good as long as there is life.

One of the reasons God created the woman was to comfort the man, and break that life of loneliness on man as in *Gen. 2:18 "it is not good for man to be alone."*

A Man needs love and to be loved, man needs encouragement. The virtuous woman shows her love not by foolish fondness.

She encourages him when out of honor.

She studies to make it easy to provide what is fit for him in health and in sickness.

She attends to him with diligence and tenderness when in ailment.

She seeks to maintain the good reputation of his family, estate property etc. not once but throughout her life.

Virtuous woman is not weary of the good offices she does to her husband. If she survives him (at the death of husband) she still does him good in the care of the children, the husband's estate, his good name and all the concerns he left behind, the right of inheritance.

Vs. 13 "She seeks wool and flax and worketh willingly with her hands."

The words used here are seek, work, willingly and develop. Her attitude to work is that of willingness, zeal and seriousness in submission, allowing her husband to make decisions and she takes responsibilities.

She applies herself with feminine business fit and appropriate (proper) to herself.

She seeks for the best and affordable materials stock ready to enable her with sufficient manufacturing.

She does not set the poor people at her work alone but she is willing to work herself as well.

She goes about her duty delightfully and cheerfully both with her hand and mind, without any weariness.

Always seeking to grow increasingly in all that she put in her business.

Vs. 14 "She is like the merchants' ship, she bringeth her food from afar."

Merchants' ship is very busy and has a lot to do, and it is full of everything. The virtuous woman has so much to do all the time. She plans her duties well to keep her house. She is indeed a busy but an organized woman. She is like a merchant's ship that travels far and wide with her products. There is always more than enough food to eat in the home.

Vs. 15 "She rises also while it is yet night and giveth meat to her household and portion to her house maids."

She makes time for her personal devotion with the Lord and seeks after *'spiritual food'* for her home.

She prays fervently to the Lord. Seeking the Lord's mighty hand in overthrowing and destroying strongholds of the enemy.

"Rises early" denotes that she seeks after supernatural food that is early morning devotion.

With the fruit of her labor, she is of great support to her family, spiritually. The house is not feeding on bread alone but also on the word of God. She sees to the spiritual growth and development of her family. She is not lazy.

Vs. 16 "she considers a field and buys it with the fruit of her hand. She planteth a vineyard."

Words like **considers**, **buy** and **plants** are used.

She is wise and reasonable in business ventures.

She takes careful consideration or planning in decision-making, especially as to the advantages and disadvantages in purchasing a land in comparison with how much funds and money she has on hand.

Out of the profits of her labor, she plants a vineyard.

In other words, makes property for her children. (Leaves a legacy)

She does not borrow. How often do we borrow from friends and even refuse to pay back?

She uses money wisely and saves for rainy days. (Future)

She buys profitable things; she buys out of necessity not on impulse.

Vs. 17 "She girds herself with strength and strengthens her arms."

That is spiritual, marital and physical fitness. Words like girds, strength and firm are used.

We are triune person just like God the Father, Son and Holy Spirit. She prepares and fills her spirit, soul and body to perform her god-given tasks. For without the power of God, she can do nothing.

A virtuous woman does whatever she needs to do with her whole heart, mind, strength and might. She does not seek to do dignified jobs only. However, she skillfully works with her hands to produce that which brings profit and she does these with all her heart.

Eph 4:28
"Let the thief steal no more but rather let him be industrious, making an honest living with his hands."

The virtuous woman is mentally fit. She has peace of mind, joy and happiness in going about her duties. She is physically fit since she takes good care of her health. She eats healthy foods; she does exercise, observes cleanliness and avoids unhealthy lifestyle that could make her fall sick. A sound mind in a healthy body will produce a successful business life.

Vs. 18 "She perceives that her merchandise is good and her light does not go out by night".

That is her gain from work is good. She sees that her work for God is a good one. By her prudence she makes good account of all her toils and does not waste time, energy and resources on vain ventures. She is indeed serious, sensible and wise in her business to make profit and increase.

Her lamp does not go out but burns continually throughout the night.

This woman stands firm in times of troubles, deprivation, and sorrow, warning and fear, doubt and distrust. Because she had Jesus as her light, the word of God as a lamp unto her feet and a light unto her path.

So she is not afraid of the perils of the night. She knows Jesus is her light in darkness.

Also it is by the mercy of God to have the candlelight to supply the want of the night when the daylight is gone. She is at work both day and night. Night or darkness does not stop her performance.

Vs. 19 "She stretches out her hand to the spindle. And her hand holds the distaff."

This virtuous woman is not boastful of her status to work. She holds on to profitable and decent work. No good work is above her honor and dignity. We need to seriously hold on to any decent, profitable work and be committed to it. We need not feel too big for certain jobs or duties, be it domestic, social and spiritual. These duties are to be done well, as unto the Lord.

Vs. 20 "She extends her hand to the poor, yes she reaches her hand to the needy."

Words like extends and reaches are used.

Extends -indicates beyond or adds more distance to her efforts in whatever she endeavors.

She is charitable to the poor, and also more close to those who are in spiritual, physical and emotional need. She does not think of getting or receiving all the time without also giving. She serves the poor with her own hand and does so freely, cheerfully and liberally with reaching hands.

Reaches here imply dedication and surety in seeking and getting to the poor to offer assistance no matter how near or far. She does well not to her neighbors and close relations alone, but also reaches forth her hand to strangers, seeking opportunities to show kindness, mercy and to communicate well.

Vs. 21 "She is not afraid of snow for her household, for all her household are clothed with scarlet."

This virtuous woman gets good warm clothing for her children and her servants. She need not fear the cold of the most pinching winter, because she and her household are well provided with clothes sufficient to keep them warm. All her family has appropriate clothes fit for winter.

She looks good with winter suit as well as summer suit.

A virtuous woman should think of having clothes for all occasions and seasons with a broad way of planning and choosing clothing suitable for different weather and occasions.

Vs. 22 "She makes for herself covering of tapestry. Her clothing is fine linen and purple."

This woman is not just a designer or a dressmaker but an interior decorator as well. She makes and designs curtains suitable for a particular place, hanging them up nicely. Linen and purple clothing signifies an executive outfit and this is her preference or choice.

Vs. 23 "Her husband in known in the gates when he sits among the elders in the land."

Due to the husband's wise counsels and prudent management of affairs, it appears that he has a discreet companion in his bosom hence he improves himself in every conversation. With cheerful countenance and pleasant humor of the man it appears he has an agreeable virtuous wife at home and not just a wife.

His clean, neat, decent attire, such handsome look, speaks of the good and virtuous wife behind him. Behind every successful man is a virtuous woman.

Vs. 24 "She makes fine linen garment and sell them; and supplies sashes for the merchants."

This woman of virtue is a manufacturer and exporter. She works so hard and is a marvelous businesswoman. She makes and sells durable and expensive clothes.

Vs. 25 "Strength and honor are her clothing she shall rejoice in time to come."

She has the satisfaction and comfort of her virtue in her own mind. She enjoys a firmness and constancy in mind. She has a strong spirit to bear up, under the many crosses and disappointments in life, which are common to all the wise and the virtuous women. She deals honorably with all people and has the pleasure of doing so therefore she shall rejoice in time to come.

She shall have comfortable, encouraging, memorable reflections that her youth was not useless. In the last days of her life, it will be a pleasure for her to think that she has a purposeful life and that she shall be rewarded for her goodness with fullness of joy and pleasures evermore.

Vs. 26 "She opens her mouth with wisdom and on her tongue is the law of kindness."

She is discreet in all her conversation. She would not talk or speak vain words, not a talkative but conscious of her words. Every word she speaks shows how much she governs herself by the rules of wisdom.

She does not only take prudent measures of herself but also gives prudent advice to others.

She is not a dictator, but with that friendly affection she makes her points clear. *"On her tongue is the law of kindness."* All she says is under the governance of the law.

The law of love and kindness is written on her heart, which reflects on her tongue. This is because she gives love to others and all she converse with. Her wisdom and kindness together put a commanding power into all she says. They command the respect and compliance of others. She is full of the *"law of grace."*

Vs. 27 "She watches over the ways of her household and does not eat the bread of idleness."

She monitors the manners of her servants that she may check how things go among them and assist them all to behave well in all things.

She makes sure they render their duties and services to one another just as Job who put iniquity far from his tabernacle and David who would suffer no wicked thing in his house. She does not interfere in the concerns of other people's homes. Her own business is what concerns her. *"Does not eat bread of idleness,"* means she is not lazy. She makes proper use of her time.

Vs. 28 "Her children rise up and call her blessed. Her husband also and he praises her."

She is a great blessing to her relations, and they offer her good words of recommendation and are prepared to recommend her to all and sundry.

Her husband is full of praises for her, because his heart safely trusts in her. She has the confidence of her husband. This is a laudable instance of conjugal love for a husband and wife to give each other, the due recognition, appreciation and praises. She receives recognition, respect and praises from all neighbors.

Ruth was recognized to be a virtuous woman:

Ruth 3:11b "For all the people know that you are a virtuous woman."

Virtue will definitely have its praise. Virtue which implies intensity, female chastity, and moral excellence. Such qualities definitely deserve praises.

Vs 29: "Many daughters have done well, but you excel them all."

Virtuous woman you are a precious jewel, as is represented in,

Proverbs 31: 10 "A virtuous woman who can find? her
price is far above rubies."

There have been many good women but such an excellent one cannot be compared to, for she excels them all.
Those that are good should aim at excelling in virtue. Many
daughters in their father's house and in single [unmarried]
state have done virtuously, but a good wife if she is virtuous
excels them all, and she does more good in her husband's
home than she can do in her father's house.

A man cannot have his house well managed and kept
by his daughters better than by an excellent wife. She shall
surely be praised.

Vs. 30 "Charm is deceitful and beauty is vain (passing) but
a woman who fears the Lord, she shall be praised."

There may be an impure deformed soul lodged in a
comely beautiful body, many have been exposed by their
beauty to such temptations and have been the ruin of their
virtues, honor and their precious souls.

> **Beauty recommends none to God, nor is it any certain**
> **indication of wisdom and goodness but it has deceived**
> **many men who have their choice of wives by it.**

Just as Solomon's definition of *"vanity"* of life. Beauty
is an addition of things at its best. Therefore it is vain and
deceitful. Just a little accident may blast this flower in its
prime. Old age will certainly wither it. Death and grave
consume it. But the fear of God reigning in the heart of a
woman is the beauty of the soul. It recommends those that
have the *fear of God* to the *favor of God*, and this in the sight

of God is a great price. [You are set to be favored if you have fear of God.]

This great virtue is indeed more precious than rubies and that makes up the virtuous woman who she is. The fear of God, a great price will last forever and bid defiance of death itself, that which consumes the beauty of the body, but consummates the beauty of the soul.

My sister, strive seriously for the fear of God for it is far more precious than your cherished beauty, clothes and ornaments, even your acquired worldly knowledge. This will attain you that mighty acclamation of the 'virtuous woman who can find?'

Vs. 31 Solomon said "Give her of the fruit of her hands and let her own works praise her in the gates."

Some women are praised but not according to their worth. But those that praise the virtuous woman do so because that is her worth. She is given that which, she has dearly earned and is justly due to her. Those who deserve praises must be given it. The fruit knows the tree it bears so if the fruits are good then the tree must have the reward.

The respect and dutiful spirit of her children, gives her the fruit of her hand. She reaps the benefit of all the care she has given them. Children must thus do their duty to reward their parents and this is showing piety at home.

She leaves it to her own works to guarantee her praise; she does not cause the applause of men. Even if her relations hold their peace, her own works will definitely praise her. No real virtuous woman loves her own praise.

Like Dorcas, goodness and praise brought her back to life. *Acts 9:39*. The widows gave the best encomium of Dorcas when they showed the 'coats and garments she had made for the poor'. Nothing should be done to hinder her praise from her neighbors.

Therefore those that do that which is good let them have praise of the same. But not to do anything enviously to diminish it but be provoked by holy emulation. Let none have an ill report from us that have a good report even of itself.

Summary of the expository of the Biblical virtuous woman:

She is a marvelous 'help meet' to her husband.
She is a victorious and successful career woman.
She is of high moral values.
She speaks with wisdom.
She cares for the poor and the needy.
Uses her money wisely, saves some for the rainy day.
Works hard to leave a legacy for her generation.
She is indeed chaste, a woman of integrity.
To crown it all, she has that great price of God-
    fearing character.
She is the woman every woman should strive to be.

OTHER PRACTICAL QUALITIES OF A VIRTUOUS WOMAN

1. She is a woman with godly vision

'**Vision**' is a form of dream, purpose or aim to achieve goals in life: A '**Vision Bearer**'.

The virtuous woman, a '*vision bearer*' should be:

Prayer burdened. She prays continually especially for men and women of God.

(I Thess.5: 7) Pray continually without ceasing

Be dependent on God. In her vision, she depends upon God for direction:

117

Prov. 3:5 "Trust in the Lord with all your heart and lean not on your own understanding."

Ps.37: 5 "Commit your way to the Lord, Trust in him and he will do it."

She is **purposeful** in her ways; hence she works to improve her talents in order to achieve her vision and purpose for her life.

Liberal: (giving) her time, finance and prayer etc.

2 Cor. 8:7 "…. Also excel in the grace of giving"
Acts 20:35 "it is more blessed to give than to receive"

Committed and hardworking to her vision:

I Kings 8:61 "but your hearts must be fully committed."

Has taken full control of her life; whole and unique:

Titus 2:4-5 "Then they can train the younger women to love their husbands and children, to be self-controlled and pure, to be busy at home, to be kind, and to be subject to their husbands so that no one will malign the word God."

2 Pet. 1:6 "Add to knowledge, self-control and to self-control perseverance, and to perseverance godliness and to godliness, brotherly kindness and to brotherly kindness, love."

Contentment: She is the type who loves to be content.

Heb 13:5 "keep your lives from the love of money and be content with what you have…"

1 Tim. 6:6 "but godliness with contentment's is great gain"

She has improved self-image: She has a positive mindset and attitude.

Eph. 4:23 "To be made new in the attitude of your minds."

Knowledgeable: She loves to study even as it is written, *"study to show yourself approved."*

2 Tim. 2:15 "Do your best to present yourself to God as one approved, a workman who does not need to be ashamed and who correctly handles the word of truth."

Humble meek and mild:

Prov. 15:33 "the fear of the Lord teaches man wisdom; humility comes before honor."

1 Pet. 5:5-6 says, "Likewise you younger ones, submit yourself unto the elder; yea all of you be subject one to another and be clothed with humility: God resists the proud and gives grace to the humble. Humble yourselves therefore under the mighty hand of God, that he may exalt you in due time."

Teachable Spirit:

She is prepared to learn more in humility and a good listener. Listening is another great virtue. [Have a listening ear.]

Prov. 11:2b "but with humility comes wisdom"

Excellent management of time and money:

She plans and has expert review proposal before executing any business or deal. She also sets her priority right.
Refuses to give up easily:

Prov. 28:1 "But the righteous as bold as lion"

She has strong **godly determination; zealous, bold never quits** whatever she plans to achieve.
"Winners never quit and quitters never win".

2. The Virtuous Woman

Has genuine faith, passing it onto her children:

Deut. 4:9 says "Only be careful and watch
yourselves closely so that you do not forget
the things your eyes have seen or let them slip from your
heart as long as you live. Teach them to your
children and to their children after them."

Deut 11:19 "teach them to your children, talking about
them when you sit at home and when you walk along the
road, when you lie down and when you get up."

Has the Spirit of Discipleship:

She teaches others, training and leading them to Christ. Right from the birth of a baby, a woman begins with the task of responsibility, nurturing and training a child the way he should go.
She has a *"broken and a contrite heart"*. She also prays for a clean heart. Has the mind of Christ in her:

Phil. 2:5 "Let this mind of Christ be in you."

Phil. 4:7-8 "and the peace of God which transcends all understanding, will guard your heart and minds in Christ Jesus. Finally brothers, whatever is true, whatever is noble, whatever is right, whatever is pure, whatever is lovely, whatever is admirable if anything is excellent or praise-worthy, think about such things".

God sees through our hearts as the mirror, and knows our ways and intentions. The virtuous woman possesses a new heart and heart of flesh not of stone.

She needs to be *filled with the fruit of the Spirit*, which are:

Gal 5: 22; Love, Joy Peace, Longsuffering, Gentleness, Faith, and Good temperance."

Rom. 8:14; "for as many as are led by the Spirit of God, they are sons of God."

What a Virtuous Woman Should Not Be:

Self-righteous or conceited, highly esteeming herself:

Phil 2:3 "Let nothing be done through strife or vain glory, but in lowliness of mind let each even esteem others better than themselves."

Not an "**I.C.E.** *woman" Independent, Capable and Efficient* She is not the *"I know it all, can handle or do it or I can do it better."*
We are all created to have fellowship and compliment each other as in:

Prov. 27:17, "Iron sharpens iron; so shall a brother brighten the countenance of a friend."

Envious, jealous, or clamorous: She does not fight for a thing that does not belong to her. She is not guilty of the evil deeds:

Gal. 5:18-19 "Now the works of the flesh are manifest; adultery; fornication, uncleanness, hatred, witchcraft etc."

Does not have *d*omineering *m*anipulative or *controlling* spirit: She does not force things to be done her way, in her wish, nor even at the expense of others.

Every woman aspiring for excellence must strife to attain these goals. Ask God to help you, He gives freely.

THREE FOLD MINISTRY OF THE WOMAN

Domestic training [as a wife and mother]
Career training [social worker]
Christian worker [a vessel or honor]

Domestic Training:

As a wife, she is trained to be respectful and submissive to her husband and extended family as well. Her marriage also extends a cordial relationship between the two families and not just between herself and the husband alone. As a mother she is trained and knows how to care, nurse, nurture and train up a child in the way of the Lord. She keeps her kitchen, bathrooms and bedrooms clean and well organized. She also knows how to cook or prepare nutritious, well-balanced meals for her family. Physical cleanliness is very important. The virtuous woman keeps proper personal hygiene of herself.

Marriage is not just for love and romance, but it is a ministry and a great responsibility, these calls for proper preparations as a good keeper of the home. You need good domestic training Details on chp.6. 'Why *women ministry in the Church.*'

Career Training:

As a career woman, you should be well mannered and responsible. You should be dedicated to your work, diligent in all that you do and always striving for excellence.

Be organized and manage your time properly. Get career training and be skillful, exhibit Christ-like attitude.

*Eccl 9:10 "Whatsoever thy hands find to do,
do it with thy might: for there is no work, nor device,
nor wisdom nor grave".*

Christian Worker:

The Christian woman as a vessel of honor should observe the rules and regulations at her work place exemplify good and Christ-like attitude, self-control and dress decently and modestly with the appropriate dress code:

*I Tim. 2:9 "I also want women to dress modestly with
decency and propriety."*

*I Peter. 3:3-5 states "Your beauty should not come from
outward adornment such as braided hair and wearing of
gold jewelry and fine clothes. Instead it should be that of
your inner-self. The unfading beauty of a gentle and quiet
spirit, which is of great worth in God's sight.
For this is the way the holy women of the past who put their
hope in God used to make themselves beautiful.
They were submissive to their own husbands."*

Like Sarah's own way of dressings.
This affected other people's lives for better. Let your life be
a book people can read.
I Peter 3:1-2 "Wives in the same be submissive to your
husbands so that if any of them do not believe the word
they may be won over without words but
by the behavior of their wives when they see
the purity and reverence of your lives:"

Details on Christian worker in chapter 8.
'The Woman that God Uses.'

TIPS FOR THE VIRTUOUS YOUNG LADY AND HER SUITOR

- Keep your heart and mind focused on God and your gaze fixed on him.
- Be strong, steadfast and forgiving. Show your suitor your integrity and honesty.
- Be confidential with his issues and protect his heart. Compliment and appreciate him when he is worthy, shake off and forgive his offenses.
- Be his cheer partner and the haven of love to him.
- Be his lover, soul mate and friend.
- Prove your commitment to his well being not of evil thoughts. Be constant in your love, it is the greatest gift a man can have.
- The best marriage partnership is one in which the partners compliment each other. One's strength compensates for the other's weakness.
- The wise woman of excellence knows that academic or financial success does not make her better than her husband.

- A virtuous lady must strive to have the ability to be a partner in a storm and a soul mate in a time of desolation.

- Have a self- controlled and dignified attitude and do not do anything that will make you look cheap.

- Let your speech be that seasoned with salt, words of wisdom and grace that edifies. Be courteous when in public.

- Let your suitor enjoy your conversation, give him the opportunity to discern and realize the valuable treasure in you. Lady you are more than riches and far above rubies.

- Be sure he is born again and willing to love and accept you unconditionally especially your temperament, physical looks, social and spiritual status.

- Be certain he loves God and desire to be used by Him. He will help and encourage your gift to promote God's work.

CHAPTER SIX

THE TWO SHALL BE ONE: MARRIAGE

Preparing for marriage:

In Christian set up, courtship is the period of time when two lovers prepare for marriage. This is the time they have concluded to come to stay together as husband and wife. Courtship in the Christian concept is not a fun making time. It is the time of serious commitment, a point of no return, with whole heart decision, to live as one forever.

This begins with a choice of the partner in the light of the scriptures with prayer and guidance. This choice cannot be outside of the Christian church or environment; a Christian should not choose a life partner who is an unbeliever.

Having confirmed the choice, the parents of the two lovers should become aware of the relationship, including the elders of the Church as well.

This must be followed by a period of a godly *'courtship.'*

Courtship /Dating:

The word *'courtship'* means the act or period of *wooing*. That is to attempt to gain the favor of a person:
by *attention* or *flattery*.

To *'woo'* means to seek the affection of a person with the intent to romance.

It also means to try to gain or achieve romance, love affair, and a romantic involvement.

'Dating' means appointment, especially: a *social* engagement between two persons that has a *romantic* character.

It also means a person with whom one has a usual *romantic* date.

'Romance' to make love or romantic attachment between lovers.

Let's consider the above breakdown or meaning of the words, *courtship, wooing, dating and romance*.

Can we deduce then that dating, courtship is an appointment/agreement to go out to socialize, an act or period to try to gain the favor of [someone] by attention or *flattery*? Is it also to seek the affection of [someone] with the intent to romance [*just* to make love] other than to pursue a quality long-lasting godly marriage or relationship?

What is one's motive, how can one ascertain the genuiness or sincerity of a partner?

I believe our *outmost* intentions and desire should seek the *right* person to live as one and share for the rest of our lives.

COURTSHIP FROM THE CHRISTIAN PERSPECTIVE

"The million-dollar question: is dating and courtship biblical? Did anybody date in the Bible?"

In this day and age we need practical counsel on courtship and *waiting* for a mate. Very little has been done to navigate the transition from proposal toward courtship and marriage. This is due to the structure and the **general gap** between [matured] old adults and young adults. We live at a time where technology, exotic lifestyle, immense promiscuity, godlessness and so many evils affect our lives making it difficult to live in *holiness* and *purity* as singles. Different people have different reasons for entering into a relationship. However, if the bottom line or end result is marriage then we need to draw the line between **marriage** and *'youthful fantasies'* with all its pitfalls of insecurities. Let us consider the following:

- Looking for love in the wrong places with unrealistic expectations.
- Putting your trust and hope in a young man or woman and not knowing what marriage really is.
- Youthful lust, selfishness, manipulation, distracting of focus, tearing down each other's purity, this is fornication.
- Are you pursuing a relationship in which the timing is wrong, the focus is sinful and has the great potential to break another person's heart?

Phil. 2:3-4 "Let nothing be done through selfish ambition or conceit, but in lowliness, let each esteem others better than themselves."

- Are you whole, complete, and unique in your singleness?
- Young man, are you ready to take on the responsibility of having a wife and raising up your children. Do you have a steady job?
- Can you provide for the needs of a family? Are you ready to be the priest of your home?

- Do you know what it means to love your wife as Christ loves the Church?
- It is all about selfless, unconditional love. Be ready to lay down your life for your bride. That is **maturity** and **readiness to marry.**
- Is your **sex drive** urging you into unprepared relationship?
- Young woman, are you ready to take on the responsibilities of having a husband?
- Do you understand what it means to submit and respect your husband?
- Are you able to take care of a home and also make a home?
- Study the skills of the virtuous woman in *Proverbs chapter 31:11-31* are you sure you are ready?
- You must be a woman who fears God. If you should date or court then a godly courtship is important.

Marriage is a c*ovenant*, **ministry** and a **mystery**, are you prepared in all aspects of life to enter into this great ministry as ordered and ordained by God?

Are you sure you can control and maintain each other's holiness and purity before the wedding day?

Are you really sure you are in **love** or in **lust**?

Are you worried about your biological clock ticking as a lady or are you under the pressure of sexual desires as a young man?

If true love is what you are pursuing, towards a godly marriage, then we need to define what *true love* really means.

True love is found in *II Corinthians chapter 13*. Most people do not know exactly what *true love* is, so we play the game of love, which is selfish, shallow, empty and wasteful. We think *love* is **sex** and **sex** is pleasure, this is far from the *truth* and against Christian values.

True Love*:* Is not what we feel; it is not the satisfaction of emotional passion. Love is all about laying down your life for one another

John 15:13 *"Greater love has no one that he lay down his life for his friends."*

Purity: Get a determined heart set in pursuit of righteousness. Respect for the beauty and sacredness of God's plan for sex in marriage.

Heb. 10:24 states *"Let us consider how we may spur one another on towards love and good deeds."*

Be determined not to tear down each other's purity and not to steal that which may belong to someone else in the future.

Remember God is holy and we must be holy. God hates sin. Sexual sin is a great rebellion and hostility against God's righteousness. In your courtship as a Christian you have a **big task** to guard and protect each other's purity, virginity and honor. As a lady, you should dress decently and protect the ***eyes*** of the guys.

I Tim 2:9-10 "I also want women to dress modestly, with decency and propriety, not with braided hair or gold or pearls or expensive clothes, but with good deeds, appropriate for women who profess to worship God."

Your value does not on your outward appearance only**, but more so in your inward beauty of a sweet and gentle spirit**.

Prov. 31:30 "Charm is deceptive and beauty is fleeting; but a woman who fears the Lord is to be praised."

Your value is in God, so fear God and respect yourself. *Watch out! It is **dangerous to take small steps in the wrong direction.** **Turn and focus on the road of righteousness.** You should see purity as a direction, a constant pursuit to please God.*

Trust: in God's Timing

Give up youthful gratification for something better. God's **timing** is the best. Trust the Lord with all your heart and lean not on your own understanding.

Trust God to provide all your needs in your singleness. See it as a chance to serve God with undivided attention, with all your heart.

I Cor. 7:32-34 "I would like you to be free from concern; an unmarried man is concerned about the Lord's affairs. How he can please the Lord. But a married man is concerned about the affairs of this world, how he can please his wife and his interests are divided.
An unmarried woman or virgin is concerned about the Lord's affair: her aim is to be devoted to the Lord in both body and spirit.

But a married woman is concerned about the affairs of this world-how she can please her husband. I am saying this for your own good, not to restrict you, but that you may live in a right way in undivided devotion to the Lord."

Do you want God's best and not your own way?
- Seek God's direction and guidance. Don't force relations.
- Don't have premarital sex. Sex is at its best when you are married, before then **abstinence** is your best choice.
- Define your relationship and set its boundaries.

- Redeem the time; *Eph. 5:15 "Be very careful, then, as how you live- not as [fools] unwise but wise."* God will surely bring His purpose to pass in **His own** time.
- Flee from your youthful lust.

II Tim. 2:22 "Flee the evil desires of youth and pursue righteousness, faith, love and peace, along with those who call on the Lord with out of a pure heart."

Count the cost of **dating** with all the **dangers** and **woes** involved. Be content with what you already have and where you are and trust in God. Be content in your singleness, do not be anxious or covet a friend's marriage. You may never know all their private challenges.

God your heavenly father knows and really cares that you get married. It is a matter of time, God's **own** *time*.

Your hope and aspirations must be channeled through God. You may be deceived by the attitudes, actions, character, qualities and values you may be looking for in a mate.

Human beings are complex.

Think seriously on how you get connected to the man or the woman of your choice. Study the following scriptures: *John 15:4-13; Prov. 3:5-6*

Have intimacy with God. *Ps. 42:1-2*

Is God the best matchmaker? *Ps. 84:11, Gen. 24:7*

Friend, choose this day what you will *trust*. Understand that the fantasies of an unprepared and incomplete man or woman are vanity. Remember also that the ever-unfailing love and providence of God remains valid. Save yourself the trouble of this *"polished fornication"*

2 Cor. 6:14-18 "Be ye not unequally yoked together with unbelievers: for what fellowship hath unrighteousness with righteousness? And what communion hath light with dark-

*ness? And what concord hath Christ with Belial or what
part hath he that believeth with an infidel? And what agree-
ment hath the temple of God with idols?
For ye are the temple of the living God; as God has said,
I will dwell in them and walk in them; and I will be their
God, and they shall be my people."*

Refuse to enter into any *covenant* partnership with an unbeliever, or a person who is not a God fearing believer.

Live as a holy person according to God's standard and principles and not that of the world. Do not get tied to them that compromise the integrity of faith and morals. Holiness must be an essential part of every relationship. Planning a marriage with an unbeliever produces an unequal alliance and that should be avoided.

To experience a happy union the believer should align with the one whose ideals and vision is centered in Jesus Christ.

God knows the woman who is called to be the *missing* rib of the man. God never makes mistakes. God is never too late or too soon. He is always *on time* and indeed at the right time. It is a matter of patience, trust and faith in Him, exercise self-control.

One's true character or the inner man cannot be and revealed or known to each other during or through dating only. The best is to rely on the sovereignty of God. He knows the mind, heart, and inner part of every man.

I also recommend you see a temperament counselor if possible for an A.P.S evaluation, and *premarital counseling*. You can contact us The *Virtuous Woman Counseling and Outreach Ministry* and we would be glad to help you, or the counseling center in your local church or a certified Christian counselor. After having been through and completed all the necessary counseling you can then proceed with your wedding arrangements.

The Right Foundation

What is the foundation or the set goal for your intention to get married? Is it your family background, position, societal status, academic achievement, wealth or beauty? Could it be the fantasies you experienced in dating? This is very deceitful.

You need Jesus to be the lamp unto your feet, and the light unto your path. You need Jesus Christ to be the solid rock as; your foundation and you will be assured of a solid firm and lasting relationship, which no storm or earthquake can pull down.

Study *Gen. 24:7* and see how God will send an angel before you to the family where your husband or wife may be, just like Isaac and Rebecca. God works in mysterious ways for His wonders to be performed, it pays to wait on Him. Pray with faith asking God for a sign.

Friend in Christ, be not wise in your eyes.

Prov. 3:5 "Lean on, trust in, and be confident in the Lord with all your heart and mind, and do not rely on your own insight or understanding."

Nuggets for the Unmarried (Single)

Definition of singleness: unmarried.
Alone - without a mate.
But not lonely - you have Christ.

The value and advantage of singleness:
Singleness is the most important state of human development. It is the foundation of God's design for humanity. [Not marriage].
God began the human race with one man [Adam]
We need foundation for every institution or life.

Adam was 'one' body; Adam 'Single' and 'Whole' before Marriage.

God 'built' Adam, the foundation of human race as a 'single person'.

Adam was to work, and keep, protect have dominion over the earth. Adam was seriously busy he never thought or dream of a wife until God saw that it was not good for him to be alone [without a mate].

Adam's singleness was before the formation of Eve and before the fall.

He was sinless, had God's image of moral nature and godly character, in the likeness [functions] of God.

He was in Eden the Presence of God: Fullness of joy, anointing, grace, strength and power.

Adam had found his self-image; he was complete, whole and unique. He had improved himself.

Before the arrival of Eve, Adam had a befitting environment or accommodation fully prepared for his wife.

God saw his dedication, commitment, hard work and righteousness; Adam was busy for the Lord in obedience and submission.

I believe God was very much impressed that He found it timely and necessary to give him a helpmeet.

So if you are unmarried get busy for the Lord:

[Seek ye first the kingdom of God...]

Do exactly as Adam did and watch God find you your mate. Get a good self-image, improve yourself, explore every potential, be the best in your area of expertise.

Singleness [unmarried] is a time for preparation for wholeness, maturity, and completion.

Tackle now the things that may be impediments in your way when you get married. The challenges ahead of you are unknown and may be far more, than you expect, so get well prepared of course in the Lord.

LAW OF MARRIAGE

So many books, lectures and seminars through the media have given a lot of information about this very delicate but sacred and important topic. It is very important because such lectures help in forming a sound, godly, successful and joyous marital life.

However some of these lectures are delicate because they have several interpretations, methods, and understanding among different people with different traditions, culture and religious backgrounds. In most cases, ignorant and less prepared people with "ghost" expectation try to work out impossible vision and desires. Worst of all, such people neglect the master minder of marriage, the one who created, ordained, purposed and planned this mystical union. These ignorant folks put aside the Almighty God.

Biblically, marriage is an institution of God. It is a ministry ordered, planned, purposed and ordained by God.

Gen. 2:24 introduces marriage.

"For this reason shall a man leave father and mother and shall cleave to his wife and the two shall be joined together as one flesh."

Love in marriage is holy God created the marriage bond. He authorized the first wedding and is the only one who can authorize a wedding today.

Gods plan for marriage was introduced: Marriage was instituted and designed by God: *Gen 2:18-25*

At the heart of marriage is the companionship and intimacy, which both husband and wife must promote: *Gen 2: 18,24*

The relationship between husband and wife is similar to that between Christ and the church. *Eph. 5:23, Eph. 5:31-32.*

A wife must submit to her husband, as the church submits to Christ. *Eph. 5:22-24*

Matt. 19:4 where Jesus said "have you not read that he who made them at the beginning made them male and female, and said for this reason a man shall leave his father and mother and be joined to his wife and the two shall become one flesh."

Exodus 22:16-17: "And if a man entice a maid that is not betrothed to him and lie with her he shall surely endow her to be his wife. If her father utterly refuses to give her unto him, he shall pay money according to the dowry of virgins"

Here virgins were protected.

"For this reason..."
The reason is that God created male and female from the beginning to be one flesh.

"Leave the father and mother ..."
This denotes parental covering, consent and blessing before marriage. It also means breaking-ties with the parents: being matured financially, socially and spiritually. It means to **leave** your parents and [**cleave to**] live with your partner.

"Be joined..."
This is passion and permanence and it denotes there is no more parental or family control, manipulation or dependency, but you and your spouse have joined together to become one flesh. Your thoughts and plans are one, joint ownership of the body, material things, sexual intimacy. Acceptance, support and respect for one another's parents and siblings when there s the need.

Hence the right order is to leave and be joined as one flesh (sexual intimacy). The best and safe place is under the covering of your parents until the fullness of your time has come for you leave and to cleave.

Caution! *Leave in respect and humility with honor for a genuine blessing* to *cleave,* to be under the covering of your spouse bearing in mind; *honor thy father and thy mother so your [marriage] days may be prolonged.* Don't cleave before the blessing *first things first.*

The New Testament word *'joined'* (according to Strong's concordance) is *'pros kollao'*, which means to glue or cement together, stick to, adhere to, joined firmly.

This word primarily describes the union of the husband and wife, the addition of pros to kollao, intensifies the relationship of husband and wife. "Pros kollao" includes faithfulness as in

Prov. 20:6 "a faithful man who can find..."

Loyalty denotes constant in devotion with regard to respect. *(Eph.5: 22-23)*

Permanence–lasting, fixed forever.

(Matt. 19:6) "What God has joined together....")

Webster's dictionary-*Marry* means to unite in wedlock, to take for husband or wife. It also means the legal union of a man and a woman.

Marriage can be termed as God's way of creating a family. He designed it to be a reflection of His nature of oneness: (Father, Son and Holy Spirit)

God is custodian of all the culture of His kingdom, godly relationship of love and unity. Marriage can be said to be

God's direction of union of the two individuals, male and female.

The Christian marriage is a four-fold mystery:

Spiritual: *Matt. 19:5, Gen. 2:24: "two shall be one"(Intimacy-sex). We are all spirit beings. The ecstasy of your spirit, your consciousness of faith in God and all the other aspects of your spirit is involved in the sex act.*

Marriage Union: That union of Christ and his bride, the Church. *(Eph 5:23-27) Marriage is a mystery.*

Biological: This is a situation where two people (husband and wife) physically become one flesh. This unity is genuine with sincere love in sexual intimacy, through which another being or child is formed in the womb and born as a living being. This is an extension of God's creative power and ability to procreate.

Social miracle: Two families are grafted together; a taste of God's intention for unity as one body and extension of His fellowship with mankind.

Who is supposed to Marry?

Any matured God fearing man or woman, who is complete, unique and wholesome–physically, spiritually, emotionally, and financially complete.

One who is gainfully, respectfully employed, and able to maintain and support himself and the family.

The man or woman, who is saved or born again with a personal relationship with Christ and is prepared to abide by the godly principles and discipline of marriage as discussed above.

How to Marry the Bible Way

Marrying in the Bible way is based on following God's principles of love and commitment. *(I Cor. 7:39)*

It is not a conditional marriage, neither is it a marriage of convenience. Rather, it goes with Agape love, guidance from God, respect to parents, and counsels from pastors and elders. Do not consummate the marriage until the wedding day. This is fornication, a sin that God hates and goes with a curse.

> *I Cor. 6:15-17 "Do you not know that your bodies are members of Christ? Shall I then take the members of Christ and make them members of a harlot? Certainly not, do you know that he who is joined to a harlot is one body with her for "the two" he say "shall become one flesh? For he who joins with the Lord is one spirit with him."*

The Bible warns about **mixed marriages:**
Do not be equally yoked with unbelievers: 2 Cor. 6:14-16

Unbelievers will lead you to sin: Exodus. 34:16, Deut 7:3-4
When men of Judah intermarried and were led into deep sin, God was angry with them. Neh. 13: 23-27.
Solomon also married foreign women who led his heart from God; he latter claimed they were all vanity.

Jesus is one with the believer in spirit. It is therefore unthinkable to involve Him in immorality.

Why Should You Marry?

It is an ideal thing and a command from God. Marriage is the most unique relationship on earth. Only in marriage do two people share their minds, their souls and even their bodies and also pledge their life-long loyalty, *"forsaking all others" as said in the wedding vows.*
God said in *Gen. 2:18 "it is not good for man be to* alone..." *[To be unmarried.]*

Man and woman are intimately related they are incomplete without one another. The woman was formed from a rib from Adam's side; the man has been born of woman, ever since.

I Cor.11: 11-12 "Nevertheless neither is the man without the woman, neither the woman without the man, in the Lord. For as the woman is of man even so is the man also by the woman; but all things of God."

We should marry:

- It is a command and God desires that men marry.
- For the continuance of God's desire to be in relationship. God desires us to see and appreciate Him in our relationships.
- For seeking and the furtherance of God's work as *Christ* and *His* bride the *Church*.
- For generational succession. [Increase and multiply]
- For the sake of human purity or sanctity to stop sexual immorality. (I Cor. 7:2-4)

I Tim 5:14 "I will therefore that the young women marry, bear children, guide the house, give none occasion to the adversary to speak reproachfully"

Gen. 3:16b "Your desire will be for your husband."
A *declaration* or bond put on woman to desire marriage except for chastity to work for God.

THE FAMILY ORDER

Christian home: *Col.3: 18-21 "Wives, submit yourselves unto your own husbands, as it is fit in the Lord. Husbands love your wives and be not bitter against them. Children obey your parents in all things: for this is well pleasing unto the Lord. Fathers, provoke not your children to anger, lest they be discouraged."*

Both husbands and wives are called to operate in God's order. A Christian renders service to others in the Lord as a way of serving Christ himself. This is how the husband and wife relationship should be. Your roles in marriage are not self-chosen nor assigned by the culture you believe in. These roles are given by God to manifest the life of Christ on earth. Both husband and wife are to submit to one another in honor to Christ.

'Submit' in Greek is *'Hypotasso'* and is formed from **'hypo'**, which means *"under"* and *"tasso"* meaning *"to arrange in an orderly manner."*

In this context it describes a person who accepts his place under God's arranged order. This submission applies to every believer.

James 4:7 "Therefore submit to God, resist the devil and he will flee from you..."

It is indeed needless to state that all these marriage principles are the best for all mankind who intend to get married, whether the person is a Jew or Gentile, Christian or non-Christian.

I Peter 5:5; "yes all of you submit yourself to one another."

Eph 5:21; "submitting one to another in the fear of God."

It is of importance to mention that it is not women alone that are bound to submit but men alike, since honoring your wife is also a form of submission and obedience to God.

Marriage is a [ministry] service unto God, your spouse, children and the nation at large. That is why broken relationship has a great impact on the society. We therefore need to practice the discipline and principles attached to God's way of marriage to have a successful marriage.

Children are to be trained to be respectful and obedient and they will not depart from it. Practiced respect and discipline in the home will have a positive impact on them. Parents must be good role models. Child and spouse abuse will affect them negatively. Fathers do not provoke your children; abuse to a child's mother in the presence of the child is definitely unbearable.

God requires parents to train their children in a God-centered way. The primary objective must be that they know, believe in, love, reverence and serve the Lord,

Parents must give biblical instructions not just lay **down rules and expectations**:

Deut.6: 6-7; John 17:3,Eph. 6:4 and Prov. 1:8-9.

The father is primarily responsible for child training. *Eph 6:4.*

DIVORCE

Divorce is one of the most drastic changes that life can bring, second only to death.

Divorce means loss of: Love and affection, Family and home, emotional support, financial stability and friends.

Marriage entails a sexual covenant. *Sexual covenants are not to be broken.*

Covenants are meant to last forever and not to be broken. That is why God hates divorce:

Mal. 2:15-16 "Has not the Lord made them one? In flesh and spirit they are His. And why one? Because He was seeking godly offspring. So guard yourself in your spirit and do not break faith with the wife of your youth. I hate divorce, says the Lord God of Israel, and I hate a man's covering himself with violence as well as with his garment, says the Lord Almighty. So guard yourself in your spirit, and do not break faith."

Any **covenant** that is violated attracts a **curse**. It is clear that when two pieces of wood are glued together they will not break in the place glued together but rather in a new place. Usually the two pieces after the split lose the original beauty and suffer damage.

That is exactly what happens to the soul, body and spirit of the individuals involved in divorce.

When two souls **cleave** together in marriage, **sealed** with **sexual intercourse**, they are supposed to stay glued together till death. This is because marriage was created not to be broken since the two have become one.

Divorce is a sin and God hates it because it is against His law. Marriage vows must be respected and kept.

Broken vows and covenants incur curses.

God speaks to the Israelites through Prophet Malachi and shows us His disapproval of the sin of divorce. *Mal. 2:14-16*

Eccl. 5:5 "Better is it that thou shouldest not vow, than that thou shouldest vow and not pay."

Whoever makes a vow binds the soul:

Num 30:2: "If a man vow a vow unto the Lord, or swear an oath to bind his soul with a bond; he shall not break his word, he shall do according to all that proceeded from his mouth."

Deut 23:21: "When thou shall vow a vow unto the Lord thou shall not slack to pay it; for the Lord thy God will require it of thee; and it will be sin in thee. But if thou shall forbear to vow it shall be no sin."

Men and women were commanded to be faithful to their vows.

Matthew 19:6; "Wherefore they are no more two but one, flesh; what therefore God hath joined together let not man put asunder."

No family member, parents, friends, no religion, doctrine, not even tradition should separate what God has joined together. What has been tied together in the presence of God should not be torn apart.

I Corinthians 7:10-13, Paul wrote "And unto the married I command, yet not I, but the Lord. Let not the wife depart from her husband: but if she departs, let her remain unmarried, or be reconciled to her husband and let not the husband put away his wife. But to the rest speak I, not the Lord: if any brother hath a wife that believeth not, and she be pleased to dwell with him let him not put her away. And the woman which hath an husband that believeth not, and if he be pleased to dwell with her, let her not leave him."

Romans 7:2-3; "For the woman which hath an husband is bound by the law to her husband so long as he lived; but if the husband be dead, she is loosed from the law of her husband. So then if while her husband lived she be married to another man, she shall be called an adulteress: but if her husband be dead, she is free from that law; so that she is no adulteress, though she be married to another man."

Mark 10:11-12; "and he (Jesus) saith unto them, whosoever shall put away his wife and marry another commits adultery against her. And if a woman shall

*put away her husband and be married to another she
committed adultery.*"

The marriage bed should not be defiled because God is
going to judge fornicators and adulterers. *(Hebrews
13:4)* Married couples have the responsibility to preserve
their intimacy from perverse and debasing practices of a
lewd society.

Understand that **divorce** must not be employed as an expedient answer to marital problems. Realize that divorce upsets,
breaks and dishonors God's intended created family order.
This attracts a curse. It brings untold hardship to the broken
homes, child delinquencies and its associated evils. It is also a
great burden on the society, nation and world at large.

So if you decide to marry, then make every effort to
marry and live within the order and the instruction given by
God. Otherwise, stay away and stop thinking about marriage
in order not to incur curses and heartaches upon yourself and
others.

The married man should be faithful, a man of integrity,
merciful and full of loving-kindness. He should be
responsible and hard working, not lazy but providing the
best of care for his family as a good husband and father.
Equally, the married woman should be virtuous, submissive
in the fear of God, hardworking and be supportive to your
dear husband and children.

Divorce brings pain, bitterness and destroys the home.
More especially it confuses the children involved and can
also destroy their future.

Make every effort to stay together; divorce should not be
an option.

After Divorce:

Divorce is a process of shock, grief and adjustments:

Challenges and solutions;
Keep in touch with family and friends.
Spend more time with your children. Explain to them,
do not blame, reassure, encourage, and let them ask
questions.
Manage your social life*; Get involved in church*
activities.
Set aside time to do something you enjoy with someone
you like.
Handling old relationship you do not really want; do
not force *a relationship you do not really want. Talk*
things over explain your feelings.
Flexibility *is the key to meeting the challenges of*
divorced life.

It is always best to seek counseling after divorce. Consider joining a support recovery group if it's available to you.

I do encourage you to stay committed to God and the things of God. Avail yourself to be used of Him, get
involved in some Christian group or activity. Find your area of gifting or talents so that you become a blessing to others and be blessed yourself all to the glory of God.

It is very important to forgive yourself and your spouse. Release the hurts to the Lord Jesus to pave the way for His forgiveness and healing. Marriage is an institution and must be built on a good, strong and solid godly foundation to guarantee a lasting relationship.

CHAPTER SEVEN

WHY WOMEN MINISTRY IN THE CHURCH

M any churches have different kinds of women ministry set up with different kinds of agendas. It is about time we know and understand what we are championing. The place of women ministry in the church from the Biblical point of view is to help women fulfill their god-given assignment on earth. To fully understand the purpose of *"Women Ministry"* in the church we need to first of all know the purpose for the creation of woman and her god-given roles to her generation as already mentioned in previous chapters.

In Titus 2:3-5, the purpose of women ministry is clearly stated. At the time of Titus, the older women who were deaconesses were mostly employed in looking after the poor and attending to the sick. But in our times, all aged women professing religion must be like the women mentioned in the verse below:

Vs.3 "Likewise, teach the older women to be reverent (respectful, graceful) in the way they live; not to be slanderous or addicted to much wine but to teach what is good. In behavior as becometh holiness."

They must accommodate their behavior to their profession. Older women are to study and learn their duties from the word, live the lifestyles that befits a spirit filled, disciplined person. They should keep a pious decency in clothing, in gesture, looks and in their speech.

They are to form an inward principle and habit of righteousness, influencing and ordering the outward conduct of others at all times:

Cor. 10:31 "Whatever you do, do all to the glory of God."

Phil 4:8 "Finally, brothers, whatever is true, whatever is noble, whatever is right, whatever is lovely, whatever is admirable-if anything is excellent or praiseworthy-think about such things."

Here we see the *"rules of conduct"* to be observed. Older women should not be false accusers, not sewers of discord, slandering and back-biting their neighbors. They should not be longing to speak ill of people and to separate very good friends. A slanderer is someone whose tongue is set on fire by hell, uttering false reports maliciously intending to injure a person's reputation. Such sins are contrary to the great duties of love, justice and equity, which spring often from malice and hatred.

A virtuous woman should get involved in such attitudes or behavior.

"Not given to much wine" denotes not drinking or not coming under the power of it. For this is immodest and shameful, it corrupts and destroys the purity both of the

body and mind. Christian older women are expected to be good teachers, having their speech seasoned with words of wisdom and full of kindness.

> *"She speaks with wisdom, and faithful instruction*
> *is on her tongue Prov. 31: 26;"*

They must indeed be teachers of good things.

> Vs. 4: *"Then they can train the younger women to love*
> *their husbands and children"*

In accordance to the command in Gen. 2:18; about a woman's duty to man, as a helpmeet, and also in confirmation of Prov. *31:11 "Her husband trusts in her."*

Younger women are to be taught by the older women in the church:

- To be trustworthy.
- To be of good personal character.
- To be sober and discrete contrary to the vanity and the rashness which the modern day youths are subject to.
- To be discrete and chaste, stand firm in their affection and behavior.
- To uphold the moral values of womanhood.

Some *concepts* of the *'Now Generation'; from a survey of some young adults:*
They are reflective, not owing responsibility.
Diverse, very inquisitive, have minds of their own.
Disrespectful; wanting respect but don't give it.
Lack foundation/ preparation: Right of Pathway.
Ill equipped spiritually and naturally.
In-patient, lazy, they want to be heard but refuse to
listen.

151

The above description of the youth given of themselves, proves how important and necessary it is for the older women to rise up, and the need for women ministries in the Churches.

Many young women have exposed themselves to fatal temptations as a result of indiscretion. One of these is **premarital sex**. More often than not this results in unwanted pregnancy and subsequent problems. Sometimes the young woman is forced to commit abortion, which is a sin in the sight of God.

'Abandoned/neglected babies' sometimes lead to child delinquencies, and eventually becomes a social liability.

Prov.2: 11 "Discretion will protect you and understanding will guard you."

The young women must be taught to be keepers of the home and care of their children. It is sad to say that women ministries in most Churches have failed to address issues like home management, pregnancy, childbirth and care.

The young women should learn to receive and care for visitors [good hospitality]. There are times young ladies enter into marriage without any knowledge, training and counseling about the above-mentioned topics.

They assume getting a partner is all that they need. It is therefore not surprising that the divorce rate is high in our generation. Mothers and Christian women, let us rise up to the call and challenge of *Titus 2:3-5*

According to *Prov.* Chapter 3 there are wonderful promises awaiting the young person who chooses God's way in which there is long life and peace.

Prov. 3 vs. 1-2 "My son do not forget my teaching, but keep my commands in your heart, for they will prolong your life many years and bring your prosperity."

This is obedience to authority and the keeping of the word of God. It releases the favor with God and you shall also have favor before men.

Prov.3: 3-4 "Let love and faithfulness never leave you; bind them around your neck, write them on the tablet of your heart. Then you will win favor and a good name in the sight of God and man."

Direction from God:

Prov. 3:5-6 "Trust in the Lord with all your heart and lean not on your own understanding; in all your ways acknowledge him and he will make your paths straight."

Prov. 3:7-8 [about health and strength.] "Do not be wise in your own eyes; fear the Lord and shun evil. This will bring health to your body and nourishment to your bones."

Prov. 3:9-10 [about abundance]: "Honor the Lord with your heart, with the first fruits of all your crops; then your barns will be filled to overflowing and your vats will brim over with new wine."

Prov. 3:13 [about wisdom for the people, who trust, honor and fear the Lord]. "Blessed is the man who finds wisdom, the man who gains understanding."

Prov. 3:14-15 [about incomparable prize] "For she is more profitable than silver and yields better returns than gold. She is more precious than rubies nothing you desire can compare with her."

The place of the Women ministry in the Church is to accomplish this command Titus 2:3-5. This confirms and shows a woman to know her place in this dispensation of grace.

Your position as a virtuous woman is a strong, spiritually disciplined, anointed, vessel of honor, who is set apart for the master's use. This position also will assist you to identify your ability, gifts, talents and responsibilities to champion the cause of Christ, for which He shared His blood to cleanse the Church; The cause of love, fellowship, sharing, caring, encouraging and holiness in the Holy Spirit.

The understanding of this positional truth will help women to study the word in order to co-rule the earth effectively. It is to enable, train both the young and the older and women to uphold the moral ethics of womanhood. It is to help women to be vision minded, to work towards the purpose and fulfillment of their vision. God has a purpose for every woman.

Jer. 1:5, which says, "Before I formed you I knew you and have set you part..."

It is to help women to find their place and fit well in society.

Build up their self-image as responsible, hardworking, humble, god-fearing wives making them loving mothers.

Women ministry in the church is an organization to *empower the woman* in all aspects of life to affect first, their personal lives and the church.

Then the home, and eventually the world: physically, spiritually, emotionally, domestically and mentally.

Women are said to be weaker vessels in the task of womanhood and motherhood, but unity through the bond of peace in Christ is strength and power.

This is why women must come together in the church to be trained, taught and equipped to be in relationship, and to compliment one another. Women ministry is part of the church body in fact a very important part, the heart of the church, without which the church cannot stand. Women should be occupied with their ministry within the things of God so that they don't waist their time in gossiping and talks that does not glorify God. (Satan finds work for the idle hands).

In most churches, women are more than 50% of the congregation; hence they form a very big asset to the church. If women are made spiritually strong and empowered in God, it will have a great positive benefit and impact on the church and on their individual lives.

Empowering women through the women ministry is empowering the church; stabilize the nation and the world at large.

Women ministries help to train future leaders, care for the elderly, visitations for the sick including pastoral care and other benevolent activities.

Women ministry should teach the young women

the rite of Pathway. Matters pertaining to the core issues of womanhood. Most especially domestic concerns of practical life.

The tone and order of women ministry in *Titus 2:3-5* is affirmed. Mothers and Christian workers, aged women, we have a task, let us therefore in the name and the strength of our Lord Jesus Christ rise up to our rights and responsibilities in the church, to teach and bring up and the young ones both spiritually physically emotionally and mentally.

In women ministry, the training of future mothers to train mothers should be our focus.

Read: Deut 4: 9, Deut 11:9.

What then is *Empowerment*?

Empower: (Webster's dictionary) is to give authority or power to, enable.

Enablement; to make able or feasible, to give legal power, capacity or sanction to divine authority [Spiritual]

Gen. 2:15 "and the Lord God took the man and put him into the Garden of Eden to dress and keep it." Dress here is from the root meaning 'to serve, work' which is 'being translated 'till' in verse 3 of Genesis. Keep means to take care or guard. So we are to work or serve [service/ ministry] to take care of God's creation.

Gen. 1:26 "Let us create man in our image, after our like- ness: and let them have dominion..."

Dominion: Due to the power we have as a result of the image of God. Supreme Authority, (Genesis 1:27) both man and woman had the same divine Image of God, which is Supreme Authority.

Matt.28: 18-19 "Then Jesus came to them and said All Authority in heaven and on earth has been given to me. Therefore Go and make disciples of all nations, baptizing them in the name of the Father and the Son and of the Holy Spirit..."

Acts 1:8 "and ye shall receive Power after the Holy Spirit had come on you..."

Who is the Holy Spirit? And what was said about Him?

Isaiah: 61: 1–3. ''The Spirit of the Lord is upon [us] because He has anointed us to preach good tidings unto the meek; he has sent us to bind the broken hearted."

Isaiah 11: 2 clearly explain the attributes of the Holy Spirit. The Spirit of wisdom and understanding, the Spirit of counsel and might, the Spirit of knowledge and of the fear of the Lord.

Before we can dress [serve] or take care or guard God's work we need to be aware that we have already from the beginning of creation been endowed with spiritual authority and power by virtue of the image of God in us.

We are therefore to 'GO' into the entire world and make disciples of nations. Our visa is the POWER from the Holy Spirit. The Holy Spirit has and can empower us with Wisdom, Understanding, Counsel, Might, Knowledge, and the Fear of the Lord. Without which we are nothing and cannot perform.

Empowerment means unity and growth.

2 Pet.3: 1 **Growth** *in the grace and knowledge of God. God promises us Spirit of Grace in Zech. 12:10. The grace we need in this grace dispensation Gal. 3:18.*

The Grace of double portion anointing,

Grace to excel in the Power of His might.

Grace to know, discern and wait on the Lord to receive strength to do exploits.

Unity love and respect through grace [unmerited favor] will bring growth.

Empowerment means Maturity, Character and Discipline.

Envy, which is jealousy of a friend's gift or achievement, may cause you to loose the little you have. Remember that you are no better than anybody but you are somebody in the sight of God.

How can Empowerment be effected?

Study the love chapter in 1Cor.13. For a healthy, firm and strong godly love relationship to accomplish your God given task.

Love and mutual respect for one another. Brothers in intended Christ unity, will enable us identify the right enemy in the midst of our battle.

Eph. 4:3-6; "Make every effort to keep the unity of the Spirit through the bond of peace..."

Unity- just as the Holy Trinity is united. The nature of this is the unity of the heart/spirit, which is the mirror of God, a broken and a contrite heart.

Phil. 2:3 "Let nothing be done through strife or vainglory but in lowliness of heart let each esteem others better than themselves"

Unity of a contrite/ broken heart, love for one another will empower us.
Eph. 4:15 "Instead speaking the truth in love, we will in all grow up into Him who is the head that is Christ Jesus" In our efforts to achieve our goals in ministry and indeed other duties in life, we are bound to meet temptations, obstacles and also fullness. And a hard lesson as it may be; that the temptations of fullness and prosperity are not less than those of affliction and want. But how must we learn and be empowered?
Empowerment lies in:

Phil 4:13 ''I can do all things through Christ who strengthens me."

Joel: 2:28-29; ''And It shall come to pass afterward, that I will pour out my Spirit upon all flesh; and your sons and your daughters shall prophesy, your old men shall dream dreams, your young men shall see visions. And also upon the servants and upon the handmaidens in those days will I pour out my Spirit."

Women have been empowered with the same Holy Ghost power on men to do God's work. There is no gender difference.
Most important of all the impact of women ministry is empowerment through Prayer.

A praying ministry is a powerful ministry. Prayer is in fact the life and the backbone of any successful ministry. The Bible calls for wailing [praying] women:

Jer. 9: 18-20.
     Effective fervent prayer will avail much.

Our strength comes from the Lord who made heaven and earth. We have need of the strength from Christ, to enable us perform not only those duties that are purely Christian, but also even those that are of moral virtue. We need His strength to teach us to be content and effective in every condition and situation. Including our ability to do a powerful and effective spiritual warfare.

CHAPTER EIGHT

THE WOMAN THAT GOD USES -
A VESSEL OF HONOR

What is a Vessel?

This is any material or an object, which may be used for any purpose.

In a person, as an agent of embodiment:

II Cor. 4:7; "But we have this treasure in jars of clay [earthen vessels] to show that this all surpassing power is from God and not from us."

Men and women who are ministers of the gospel are instruments for God; they are but His *earthen vessels*. They carry the *Treasure*, which is the *gospel* of light, truth, and grace that has been *imparted* in them.

Timothy discusses this vessel:

II Tim. 2:19-23 "Nevertheless the foundation of God is sure, having this seal, The Lord knows them that are His. And let every one that names the name of Christ depart from iniquity".

Vs. 20 "But in a great house there are not only vessels of gold and of silver, but also of wood and of earth; and some to honor and some to dishonor."

Vs. 21" If a man therefore purges himself from these, he shall be a vessel unto honor, sanctified and meet for the master's use and prepared unto every good work."

Vs.22 "Flee also youthful lusts: but follow righteousness, faith, charity, peace, with them that call on the Lord out of pure heart".

Vs.23 "Do not have anything to do with foolish and stupid arguments because they produce quarrels."

Paul says in *vs.19*

That the promise of God cannot be made ineffective by the unbelief of man. The overthrow of people's faith cannot shake God's foundation.

No attack of the powers of darkness on the word of God and doctrine of Christ can shake **The Truth**, *which is* Christ Jesus. He became the ***foundation***. [***Seal***]

Vs. 20 The Church of Christ is a ***great house*** well

furnished. Some of the furniture is of great value and others are of lesser values. In the Church there are ***vessels*** of honor and dishonor. There are also ***vessels*** of mercy and ***vessels*** of wrath.

Rom. 9:22-23 says "What if God, willing to show His wrath and to make his power known, endured with much long-suffering the vessels of wrath fitted to destruction: and that he might make known the riches of his glory on the vessels of mercy which he had afore prepared unto glory".

There are **vessels** of **noble** and **ignoble** purposes. Those of **noble** purpose are made holy, sanctified, cleansed, useful, adopted and prepared for good use by the Master.

Ignoble vessels are dishonorable, shameful, disgraceful, sinful, and useless to the Master.

Friend which of these **vessels** are you made up of? Every one must strive to be a **vessel** of **honor** and of a **noble** purpose; we must **purge** our selves (hearts) from corrupt opinions that we may be **SANCTIFIED** for our great Master's use. Every one in the Church of God should be devoted and useful to His service.

Sanctification (**cleansing, purging**) of the *heart* is our preparation for every good work. The tree must be good so that the fruit will be good.

The path to **holiness** and **purity** comes in two ways:
These are *obedience to God-* **'Matt 7:21-24'**
[Doing **the will** *of the Father]* remember **disobedience** *brought the* **curse.**

And *consecration* **to God-** *'Rom, 8:29'*
[Predestinated to be conformed to His Image…]
Have a sincere heartfelt repentance; God is not interested in public demonstration of piety.
Read Matt 6: 16-18
God is rather looking for people who will turn their hearts to Him in humility and meekness. So that they may receive His forgiveness, be purged and made a vessel of honor meet for His use.
Check these scriptures:

Ps 51:10; "Create in me a clean heart, oh God; and renew a right spirit within me."

Prov.4: 23-24 "Guard your heart for it is the well-spring of life. Put away from thee a froward and perverse lips put far from thee. Let thine eyes look right on and let thine eyelids look straight before thee."

.Joel 2:13 also says "Rend your heart and not your garment…"

*Heb. 12:14; **"Follow peace with all men and holiness without which no man shall see the Lord."***

Rom.12:1 says "I beseech you therefore, brethren, by the mercies of God, that ye present your bodies as a living sacrifice, holy, acceptable unto God, which is your reasonable service."

I Peter. 1:15; "As he who hath called you is holy, so be ye holy in all manner of conversation."

I Peter 1:18-19 says "For as much as ye know that ye were not redeemed with corruptible things, as silver and gold, from your vain conversation, received by tradition from your fathers; but with the precious blood of Christ, as a lamb without blemish and without spot."

There are always going to be some hindrances on our way to holiness:

SOME HINDRANCES TO HOLINESS

In **Leviticus chap. 16** *we* learn of the Ark of covenant with the **veil** separating two **realms; the Holy place from the**

Holy of *Hollies* the *Visible and the Invisible; physical and spiritual [symbol of God's presence] Heb 9:12-17*

This signified separation since none but the high priest could pass beyond the most sacred place, and he only on the Day of Atonement. The veil was rent at the time of the crucifixion to show that now all men could freely come to God. The Apostle Paul speaks of the veil of ignorance, blindness and hardness of heart, which kept the Jews from understanding the scriptures of the Old Testament, the spiritual sense and meaning of the law and from seeing that Christ is the end of the law for righteousness. [*John 9:39*].

Veil here signify *barriers* [sin *and hindrances].*

We cannot enter the Holy of Holies through the *veil* unless something happens to these eyes of the *flesh*; *2 Kings 6:17.*

*Rom. 8:23*We have a *barrier* in our *flesh*, hence the cry for *redemption* of our body.

We must *experience and maintain* our salvation, sanctification and redemption through the *blood* of the risen Savior.

There are 3 veils in our lives, *flesh, mind, and heart.*

These veils keep us out of the holy of holies [presence and, fellowship with God]

THE THREE VEILS

The veil of the flesh:

1 Thess. 4:4 "Every one of you should know how to posses his vessel in sanctification and honor."

Heb 10:20 "By a new living way, which He had consecrated for us through the veil that is to say His flesh."

Thomas had a veiled heart as well as veiled flesh. He was of a very doubtful heart and flesh.

John 20:29. "Then Jesus told him, because you have seen me you have believed; blessed are those who have not seen and yet have believed."

Gal. 5:16 "This I say then, walk in the Spirit, and ye shall not fulfill the lust of the flesh."

The Veil of the Mind:

*2 Cor. 3:3:14 "**But** their minds were blinded for until this day remaineth the same veil untaken away in the reading of the Old Testament; which veil is done away in Christ."*

2Cor 4:3-4; "In whom the god of this world hath blinded the minds of them which believe not, lest the light of the gracious Gospel of Christ, who is the image of God, should shine unto them."

The Veil of the Heart:
God wants unveiled hearts:

2 Cor.3: 12-18 "Seeing then that we have such hope, we use great plainness of speech. And not as Moses, which put a veil over his face that the children of Israel could not steadfastly look to the end of that which is abolished. But their minds were blinded for until this day remaineth the same veil untaken away in the reading of the Old Testament; which veil is done away in Christ. But even unto this day, when Moses is read, the veil is upon their heart.

Nevertheless, when it shall turn to the Lord, the veil shall be taken away. Now the Lord is that Spirit, and where the Spirit of the Lord is there is liberty.
But we all, with open face beholding as in a glass the glory of the Lord are changed into the same image from glory to glory even as by the Spirit of the Lord."

The three veils stands for the sins of our heart, flesh and mind, which are hindrances separating us from the presence and glory of God. We need to break our hearts, renew our minds and crucify the flesh.

We have access to the Holy of Holies through: Worship, Brokenness, Restoration and Spiritual Nakedness.

ACCESS TO THE HOLY OF HOLIES

Two Things that brings us through the veil

Worship:

John 4:24 "God is spirit and His worshippers must worship Him in spirit and in truth."

Matt. 4:10 "Worship the Lord your God and serve him only."

Brokenness:

Psalm 51:17 "The sacrifice of God are a broken spirit: a broken and contrite heart, O God, thou wilt not despise."

Joel 2:12 also "Even now declares the Lord, return to me with all your heart with fasting and weeping and morning. Rend your heart and not your garment. Return to the Lord your God for he is gracious and compassionate..."

Rend [tear apart] here implies repentance where we are greatly grieved in the soul for sin so that it even cuts to the heart.

All that the Lord needs from us is thanksgiving, obedience and humility. Sincere praise and worship.

Through *Spiritual Nakedness*: [a form of brokenness] There is a revelation of nakedness in *Gen. 3:9*.

We learn of Adam and Eve's sin, which brought nakedness.

In *Matt. 27:28*, our Lord and Savior Jesus Christ who is the second Adam was also striped *naked*.

What is the significance of this nakedness to our lives? What at all is *nakedness*? It is exposure, without any clothing.

Nakedness Rev 3:17 "Because thou sayest, I am rich, and Increased with goods, and have need of nothing; and knowest not that thou art wretched, and miserable and poor and blind and naked."

-without body or the preparation of **the inner man.**

The inner man implies our soul and heart; are without house and the harbor of our soul without the garment of justification and sanctification.

In other words, the heart and soul of man are without the garment of *righteousness*. It implies that the *nakedness* of *guilt* and *pollution* of man has no covering.

The eyes of both Adam and Eve were opened under the consequences of sin. Hence, they realized they were *naked* and sewed fig leaves to cover their *nakedness*. Sin brought about an eye opener to them, a realization of their *nakedness*. Their "eyes were opened" means their conscience became alerted. They had lost all the glory, honor and comfort they had. The conscience is the storehouse of both evil and good thoughts.

Nakedness here is exposure, having no covering for sin and shame. *Sin* and *shame* in our *nakedness* is dishonor. It brings mischief and embarrassment whenever it is admitted and sets men against themselves. It is capable of disturbing their peace and destroys all their comforts. Sin and shame and nakedness take away one's glory, gracefulness and integrity, which make him feel very much degraded. Thus was how Adam and Eve felt after sinning. This is exactly how we feel when in sin and we come short of God's glory.

But the good news is that the shame and *nakedness* ends with true *repentance* to the praise and glory of God.

Which results in an individual being cleansed and covered with God's *righteousness*.

After Adam and Eve sinned, God covered them with coats of skins. Sin is indeed a reproach. Adam and Eve made aprons out of fig leaves to cover part of their shame. But God's provision of the coats of skin was to signify the coming of the second Adam (the lamb that was already slain before the foundation of the earth, even Jesus Christ, who is God's righteousness.

The common folly, ignorance of those that have sinned; is that they are more willing to show their credits before men than to obtain their pardon from God.

They are reluctant to confess their sins but will do whatever it takes to conceal such sins; *"I have sinned yet honor me."* The excuses men make to cover and extenuate their sins are vain and frivolous. Like in the making of aprons of fig leaves, Adam and Eve were never able to conceal their sins, but rather the hidden sins with time become even more shameful. Most people are apt to harbor their transgression.

Job 31:3, "Is not destruction to the wicked? And a strange punishment to the workers of iniquity?"

The wicked will definitely pay for their sins. We reap what we sow, whether good or bad; but the good news is that there is forgiveness when we sincerely repent and turn from our wicked ways.

When there is sin or shame, our true **repentance** and **nakedness** before God brings His **covering** of **righteousness** and **holiness**.

God restores the sinner to the lost grace and honor after true repentance.

Joel 2:25: says "And I will restore to you the years that the locust hath eaten, the cankerworm, and caterpillar, and the palmer worm, my great army which I sent among you."

Ps. 51:12 says "Restore unto me the joy of thy salvation: and uphold me with thy free spirit."

Zech. 12:10 "And I will pour upon the house of David and upon the inhabitants of Jerusalem the Spirit of grace and of supplications..."

Beloved it is better and expedient not to conceal our sins but to bring our **nakedness [sins]** before God for **cleansing** and **healing**.

Let us consider *Jesus' nakedness:*

Matt. 27:28; "They striped him naked and put a scarlet robe."

Shame of nakedness came on Him with our sins:
Therefore when Christ came, was made naked after which He satisfied the conditions for sin and took it away.

Christ submitted to that shame so that He might prepare white raiment to cover us.

Rev. 3:18 says "I counsel thee to buy of me gold tried in the fire, that thou may be rich and white raiment, that thou mayest be clothed and that the shame of thy nakedness do not appear; and anoint thine eyes with eye salve, that thou mayest see."

Jesus Christ the king of kings and the Lord of Lords was striped physically naked.

He put down all His reputation and kingship. He endured the shame, disgrace and the dishonor and was subjected to the most dehumanizing situation because of our sins.
(Phil. 2:5-8)

He in turn has given us salvation and as joint heirs with Him, a place for us in God's glorious Kingdom.

We need not go physically naked as was done to Christ or what Adam and Eve realized. Instead we are to part with sins and self-sufficiency and come to Christ with a sense of **need** and **emptiness (nakedness)** that we may be filled with His treasure.

That is His own imputed **righteousness** for **justification** and the garments of His holiness and the **fear of God**. We need not also stay in sin while grace abounds. Our sinful and shameful conscience must be exposed before God, for **cleansing** and **restoration**. Our **nakedness** cannot be concealed. It is time to come out boldly and not be ashamed of your sins, shortcomings and filth before the righteous and ever merciful God.

Rom. 6:14-16; "For sin shall not be your master, because you are not under law, but grace. What then? Shall we sin because we are not under law, but under grace? By no means! Don't you know that when you offer yourselves

171

*to someone to obey him as slaves, you are slaves to the one whom you obey- whether you are **slaves to sin,** leads to **death,** or to **obedience,** which leads to **righteousness?"***

*Rom. 6:22-23 "But now that you have been **set free from sin** and have become **slaves to God.** The benefits you reap leads to **holiness** and the result is eternal life. For the wages of sin is death, but the gift of God is **eternal life** In Christ Jesus our Lord."*

Joel 2:13 says "Rend your hearts and not your garments and turn unto the Lord your God: for He is gracious and merciful, slow to anger and of great kindness and repenteth of evil."

Such boldness shames the devil and rebukes the demonic spirit out of your life. It displeases Satan because he knows there is deliverance and freedom for you when his grounds in your life are exposed. When you cover your sins you increase your guilt and shame even though you may feel comfortable.

When our ***nakedness*** is exposed we open up for repentance, confession, forgiveness and total deliverance. This way we get closer and become intimate with God. He restores us.

Joel 2:25: "And I will restore to you the years that the locust hath eaten, the cankerworm, and caterpillar, and the palmer worm, my great army which I sent among you."

Ps. 51:12 says "Restore unto me the joy of the salvation: and uphold me with thy free spirit."

God then fills us with the Holy Spirit and empowers us, gives us spiritual gifts to do His work. He is then able to use us as "vessels of honor."

SPIRITUAL GIFTS:

Through **Spiritual Gifts**: God has given every person a special gift. It is up to each person to find out what his gift is and develop it. As we surrender and avail ourselves to God, He works in us and with us and through us.

Paul describes some of the various gifts in:

Rom 12:6-8 "Having then gifts differing according to the grace that is given to us, whether prophecy, let us prophesy according to the proportion of faith, or ministry, let us wait on our ministering; or he that teaches, on teaching; or he that exhorted, on exhortation; he that gives, let him do it with simplicity; he that rules, with diligence; he that shows mercy, with cheerfulness."

These are gifts given by the Holy Spirit to individuals in the church to build up God's people. They are given to us to compliment one another in the body of Christ.

Let your strength balance the weakness of others, and vice versa. Let us all be grateful that other people's abilities make up for the deficiencies in us. In the table on the next page we will see some of these gifts, seek the face of God, identify your gifts and use them to the glory of God; and the edification of your brethren in the body of Christ.

SPIRITUAL GIFTS OF WOMEN IN THE BIBLE

Spiritual Gift	Scripture Reference	Function	How to Recognize	Gifted Woman
Prophecy	Luke 2:36-38	Proclamation in order to edify	Ability to address audiences with inspired message	Anna
Serving (Ministry, Helps)	Luke 4:38,39	Service	Joy in doing for others and meeting needs	Peter's Mother-in-Law
Teaching	Acts 18:24-28	Instruction that is understood	Understanding difficult matters: ability to deliver instruction effectively	Priscilla
Exhortation	John 4:28-30	Persuasion and encouragement	Ability to inspire and persuade	Samaritan Woman
Giving	Luke 21:2-4	Under girding and supporting	Joy in giving, expecting nothing in return	Widow with Two Mites
Leading (Administration)	Judges 4:4-14	Administration	Organized; inspires cooperation and teamwork	Deborah
Mercy	Acts 9:36-42	Tender sensitivity	Concern for those who are being hurting	Dorcas
Wisdom	Luke 1:46-56	Application of truth	Ability to apply knowledge and understanding to life situations	Mary of Nazareth

Spiritual Gift	Scripture Refcrence	Function	How to Recognize	Gifted Woman
Knowledge	1 Sam 2:1-10	Insight and perception	Understanding of facts and situations	Hannah
Faith	Matt. 15:21-28	Optimism and confidence	Confidence in the Lord and ability to inspire others	Syrophoen-cian woman
Discernment	1 Sam. 25:2-42	Ability to make judgments	Ability to determine good or evil and see beyond surface	Abigail
Evangelism	Acts 21:9	Ability to witness in any situation	Loves people; talks easily; rejoices to share Christ	Philip's Daughters
Hospitality	John 12:1-2	Assistance and service	Unselfish desire to meet the needs of others	Martha
Speaking	Ex. 15:20,21	Talks easily and inspires others	Likes to talk; interested in others	Miriam
Celibacy	Acts 16:11-15	Devotion	Content to remain single	Lydia (possibly single)

Most people have some of the gifts and not all. An assertive person may not be a good counselor, and a generous giver might fail as a leader. [*Difference in temperaments*] On the other hand it would not be difficult for one person to embody all these gifts. Though everyone has a *gift,* it is possible some can have it all. Find out *how* to use your *gift* for the edification of the brethren in the body of Christ.

Become a fruitful vessel of honor for the Master's use.

CHAPTER NINE

SOUL-TIES: MATTERS OF THE HEART MIND AND EMOTIONS

What is a Soul-tie?

The *soul* constitutes one's mind, emotions and will. *Tie* means to be bonded, knit or tied together.

Soul–tie therefore exists whenever there is relationship between two people and their souls are tied together into a kind of unity.

Every association and relationship is possible since the souls of the people involved have entered into a covenant or an agreement to do so.

Soul-tie is the bond between two parties in the realm of the *soul*, (mind) which eventually has its place in the *heart* where the will of man is.

Whatever finds its way to the heart will affect the emotion in some ways. However, since it is difficult for one to see into the soulish realm it makes such issues very sensitive and at times dangerous.

For instance, we become soul-tied to blood relations due to birth and also *soul-tied* to people we work and live with. There is an equally strong tie between people we associate and those whose leadership we submit as it is in the case of a pastor and his congregation, company employer and the employees, friend's etc. A soul-tie can be good or bad, healthy or unhealthy.

There is a Godly-soul-tie, which is good, and there is an ungodly soul-tie, which brings sorrow, suffering, misery, confusion, disappointment, destruction and even death.

Godly Soul- tie

God the good Creator has set principles that should regulate and govern human relationship and behavior.

These principles reveal basically the, **will purpose** and **plan** of God, for people at any given situation and circumstance in life. Whenever a relationship is established according to biblical standards and within the framework of the plan and purpose of God, such relationship is godly. So the soul tie established is a godly and holy one. The basis of this is **Agape Love** and God's blessings are found in such healthy relationship. The **Covenant of Salvation** and **Fellowship** endear man to be **soul-tied** to God.

Deut. 10:20 "Thou shall fear the Lord thy God; him shall thou serve, and to Him shall thou cleave, and swear by His name."

Cleave is used in place of **knit**. It is used to describe relationship through soul-tie. According to *Strong Exhaustive Concordance*.

God wants man to come closer to Him, to follow close after Him, to be attached to Him and to adhere to Him as with glue or any adhesive material.

The covenant of salvation joins us to the Lord and makes us one with him.

1 Cor. 6:17 **"He who is joined to the Lord is one Spirit with Him"**

The believer's mind is also joined with Him in the covenant of salvation. The stronger the soul-tie between God and the believer is, the greater his desire to do God's bidding and fulfills His plans through his thoughts, purpose and desire.

We can be able to respond to God's love towards us and love Him because our emotion is joined to His.

1 Cor. 2:16 "We have the mind of Christ."
Deut. 6:4 "Hear, O Israel the Lord our God is one.
*You shall love the Lord with all your heart and with all your **soul**."*

1 John 4:19; "We love him, because He first loved us."

Godly soul-tie or intimacy nourishes and unites us, enhances our lives, it brings us liberty and invigorating life experiences. It is freedom *joy and peace*.

An example of a godly soul-tie is that between David and Jonathan, *(1 Sam. 18:1-4)* this brings mutual benefits to the persons involved, this made Jonathan part of David's army.

Ungodly Soul-tie

We just learned about Godly soul-tie, Agape love is the basis of godly soul-tie, and it works with Biblical principles within the framework of God, the opposite is ***ungodly***

soul-tie. Any relationship therefore which does not have its foundation on Agape love with the revealed will of God's plan is ungodly and God's blessing is not in it.

Broken vows, promises or agreements at times leaves people with hurt, pains and moral failures. Women are most vulnerable and victims in such situations. Some for years find it difficult to forgive and forget. They feel their integrity; love and trust have been abused and betrayed. Women need to be encouraged and assured of Christ's continued and everlasting love.

Ps 27:10, "Though my father and mother forsake me the Lord will receive me".

If the whole world should forsake you, God will not and anytime you are forsaken it is then time for God to take you.

Before we can wage war effectively on the kingdom of darkness, we must first recognize the spiritual war raging within each of us. In the spiritual realm, there are gates to our spirits, soul and body. The child of God's gates are sealed by the Holy Spirit, but we can leave these gates open by what we do such as holding on to past sins, negative confessions and pronouncements of curses. In order to be effective Christians we ought to guard our heart, which has our mouths as its door.

Prov. 4:23; "Above all else, guard your heart, for it is the wellspring of life."

Ps. 39:1 also states "I said, I will watch my ways and keep my tongue from evil."

Peter Horrobin says, "Problems associated with ungodly soul-tie are enormous, and can only be solved through repentance, confession, forgiveness and forgetfulness of the past hurts."

Ungodly soul-tie is established through sins such as fornication, lust, adultery, lesbians, homosexuals, sexual abuse, rape, incest, oral and anal sex (sexual perversion), also witchcraft, manipulation, control and domineering. Note that God and his word do not approve any in the above listed sins. Any relationship in this category is ungodly.

There are about five different areas of godly and ungodly soul-ties:

Ungodly soul-tie within the family;

Ungodly soul-tie inside the marriage;

Ungodly soul-tie through abuse of free will and ungodly soul-tie through witchcraft control.

But our focus shall be on the soul-ties in sexual relationship.

Dangers in Ungodly Soul-ties:

Many people are genuinely born again and cleansed by the precious *blood* of *Jesus*. Yet they remain in a type of bondage in their mind (thoughts) concerning the hurts and pains of the past. The ungodly soul-tie is due to personal covenants (covenantal relationship) with sexual partners and close relations.

Such sins separate us from God, we loose God's grace and glory and the chance to inherit heaven.

Rom 3:23 "for all have sinned and fall short
of the glory of God."

We loose the presence of the Holy Spirit and His blessings. Ungodly soul-tie is a *poisoned spiritual life*, which will make your life stunted and result in backsliding. Like Solomon who lusted after many foreign women, as the Bible says; they turned his heart from God. *(I Kings 11: 16)*

Believers should be careful whom they marry. Do not be unequally yoked with unbelievers. Any sex act done within the framework of proper marriage, God receives it as a form of a blessed covenant.

When the opposite happens, Satan comes down to receive it and curse the couple with so many things including heartbreaks, bitterness, generational marital problems and sicknesses. Satan sends down a demon to keep the cursed covenant.

Mind you, Satan uses this means to steal the joy, happiness and the peace in your marriage. He uses it to destroy your glory, honor, integrity and respect. A broken relationship will leave you with all the problems attached to it, confusion, depression, and bitterness and sometimes can lead to death.

Memories of certain people in past relationships bring fresh hurts and bitterness to your minds.

In all these, women are most vulnerable. The bitterness and unforgiving spirit over the past jeopardize our joy, peace and growth in the Lord. These memories can also put fear and doubt in people to enter any other relationship in the future.

SEX-THE STRONGEST HUMAN COVENANT

The most sacred and highest form of soul-tie covenant between two living persons is the marriage covenant in which the two souls are inextricably tied together. This covenant is consummated with sex.

What makes the marriage strong is the principle of cleaving where the two are no longer two but one flesh.

The subject of sex and sexuality is one area less taught or discussed in the church, yet it is the one area that most are held in bondage.

Thank God for the provision of repentance and forgiveness. But it is sad to say that the plaguing memories and hurts of such relations remain even after your conversion.

Many do not know that the dangers of ungodly soul-tie through unhealthy relationship could torment them if not confessed, renounced, forgiven and forgotten.

The difficulty many have is that when they broke the relationships with their sexual partners long before they became born again Christians, and can't believe the soul-tie still exists with attending dangers.

All the 3 [spirit, soul and body] faculties of your being were involved in that sex act so if there was physical separation there must be the soul's and spirit's separation as well: This is the ***breaking of the soul-tie.***

I Cor. 15:44b "if there is a natural body there is also a spiritual body."

Sexual immorality is not fun games. Since it is done outside the will of God, Satan knows that those people are disobeying God so he sends down curses like incurable diseases, lustful spirits, emotional pains, heartbreaks etc. God's plan, purpose and gift of sex do not bring such hardship on people.

The Bible makes it plain the enormity of sexual sins and says that the fornicator and adulterer sins against his own body, which is the temple of God, and He (God) will destroy the man or woman involved. Sexual sins defile not the body alone but the soul and spirit as well: wherein dwells the Spirit of God and is against the image of God.

This defilement is not necessarily the contractions of physical diseases like gonorrhea, syphilis and the horrible AIDS scourge. But there is a deadly defilement in the realm of the spirit as well, transference of spirits.

[Acquired Indefinite Destruction Syndrome- A.I.D.S] Spiritual energies both positive and negative are transferred along soul-ties. Many people might have had more than two

sexual partners imagine how 'fragmented' and defiled their souls would become.

1Cor 6:18 "Flee fornication. Every sin that a man doeth is without the body but he that committeth fornication sinneth against his own body."

Ignorance is no excuse in spiritual matters. It is of great importance that the young and the old alike control their sex drive. After confessing your sins you need to break the covenants [un-godly soul-ties] mention specific names and ask God to cleanse the pollution that have resulted from these sins of immorality with the blood of Jesus. Forgive yourself and clear your mind from all guilt, receive cleansing and maintain your deliverance. You can also seek counseling or help from an anointed man of God with a proven ministry.

You must understand that *sex* is a three-fold mystery: *physical*, *biological* and *spiritual*.

Physical: Sex act is between man and woman.

"Therefore a man shall leave his father and mother and be united to his wife and they would become one flesh."
(Genesis 2:24)

Biological: It involves the exchange of the most treasured substances of life. In sexual act when the *hymen* is broken for the first time, the blood of the woman and the semen of the man were mixed to seal the covenant. The *HYMNAL* blood of the woman is the blood of a living person and the semen contains sperm, which are the highest form and the seed of life. There is nowhere [no other instance in life] in the world can there be any covenant as *unique strong and sacred*, as the *sexual covenant*.

There is *life* and **death** in the **blood**. This implies that in life till death do you part.

Soul-ties [sexual covenant established] in sexual intercourse either *'legal'* or *'illegal'* are most difficult to break. Especially with the first sexual partner who breaks the hymen. This is because:

Genesis 3: 16 states "And your desire will be for your husband, and he will rule over you."

- In the case of the unmarried, her first sexual partner.

Whoever has the first sexual encounter with a woman exercises a kind of dominion over her. Separation or divorce does not destroy the soul-tie and the covenant still remains until all sins are confessed and forgiven, through the precious blood of Jesus Christ. The individuals should go through deliverance and break the soul-ties in the name of Jesus. Seek an anointed minister with a proven ministry.

It therefore becomes necessary for both men and women to take control of their sexual lives.

Spiritual: sexual act is not just a fleshly union but also a spiritual act.

Gen4: 1. Describes the sexual act between man (Adam) and woman (Eve).

"And Adam knew his wife."

The same Hebrew word used to describe sexual intercourse in the Bible is the same used to describe man-knowing God.

This makes sexual relationship spiritual, sacred and beautiful it can also be dangerous and deadly as well because. If it is done within the framework of proper marriage, God comes down to receive it as an act of worship and blesses it. The opposite happens in an 'illegal' sex through ungodly soul-ties, Satan receives it and curses those involved [fornicators adulterers and any sexual sins.]

God blesses 'legal' sex covenant and Satan curses 'illegal' sex covenant.

Sexual Sins Destroys:

I Corinthians 6:18-20; "Flee fornication. Every sin that a man doeth is without the body but he that commits fornication sinneth against his own body. What? Know ye not that your body is the temple of the Holy Ghost, which is in you. Which ye have of God and ye are not your own? Ye are bought with a price therefore glorify God in your body and in your spirit which are God's."

I Cor. 3:16-17; "Don't you know that you yourselves you are God's temple and that God's Spirit lives in you? If anyone destroys God's Temple, God will destroy him. For God's temple is sacred and you are the Temple."

Other references about sexual immorality:
Why sex must be limited to marriage:
Gen. 1:28 Heb. 13:4 1 Cor. 7:5
Sexual desire must be placed under God's control:
I Thessalonians 4:1-8, Gal. 5:16-18 2, Tim. 2:22
Why God forbids sexual sins:
I Cor.6: 13; 1 Cor. 10:8; Eph 5:3
Why sexual temptation is difficult to withstand:
I Cor. 7:25-27 Rom. 7:13-20

Why sexual sin is so dangerous:
Lev. 20:10-20, Prov. 5:21-23, 1 Cor. 10:8
Consequences of sexual sins are devastating:
1 Thess. 4:3-8, 1 Cor. 6:9-10
Spiritual surgery may be needed to avoid sexual
immorality: Matt 5: 29-30

You can overcome sins of sexual immorality:
Prov. 4:23-27

The natural passion and desire for sex [sex drive] is a gift given by God for a sacred and precious purpose. Misuse and abuse of it will cause one more than the 'supposed pleasure'. Save yourself the trouble.

Precious woman, created in the holiness and purity of the image of God, bought with the precious blood of Jesus, be careful to preserve your *"pure original state."* A man should be very careful not to break the virginity of a young woman who is not his wife, or indulge in sexual immorality for fun, in order not to stay under a curse or defile God's temple, which is your body.

This is *sanctity* to human life:
The natural passion and desire for sex [*sex drive*] is a gift given by God for sacred and precious purpose. It must be used in the right purpose, plan and time of God, which becomes a blessing. It is indeed a good thing, a *powerful source* of life and *unity* between two beings.

However, if it is outside of God's plan, it quickly becomes a means of *division*, a *source* of *cruelty*, *perversion* and even death. Outside of hunger, the most powerful of all human urges is the *sexual appetite*.

Satan seems to use this tool because other temptation does not work. The sexual desire becomes intertwined with our natural need for love, acceptance, belonging, caring and tenderness.

The trap is laid and many Christians are falling into it, just like those outside the Christian community. A drive for food, water etc. must be satisfied in order to survive so it is with *sex drive. It can destroy us if we let* it run out of control.

Sex is not a *goal* it's a gift, the chief goal and purpose of life is to honor and glorify the Lord with your body.

Illicit sex cannot provide the joy that one desire from God. Peace, joy, inward satisfaction is often confused for *sexual* pleasure.

Friend be careful of how, when, and for what reason you use this *powerful gift.* Inner joy is where there is no sin; it is possessed by the pure in heart.

This kind of joy is true, unselfish; it is *love* -the perfume of holiness and purity.

Child of God, it pays to wait for God's precious and perfect time. Stay away from the pollution of the media: TV, Internet, magazines and pornographic materials.

Sexuality and Spirituality:

Let us look more into sex and the spirit life. This is a very important issue, but less thought of by people. In the first place how does your sexual behavior affect your relationship with God? Know that sex is interrelated with your spirit because of the involvement of your soul and the Holy Spirit dwelling in you. Sex causes two persons to commune with one another on the deepest level of their being and commune with God at the same time.

Remember that without God's breath of life and image in man, (men and women alike) man will be nothing but dust, a mortal being. It is impossible for two [mortal beings without the breath of God] dead bodies to have sex.

It is in Him we live, move and have our being. In the Old Testament God showed His people that their sex life and spiritual life affected one another, so many regulations were laid down about marriage and sexual immorality.

The book of Leviticus contains very interesting laws that reveal the tie between the sexual and spiritual. For example, Leviticus 15 prohibits a man from worshipping at a temple if he has recently had sexual intercourse or if he had touched a woman during her menstrual period, read *Lev15: 16-19.*

Our bodies together with the soul and spirit work in unison during sex act just as in any other action. You cannot separate your spirit [that which communes with God] from your body in sex act.

Consider this that man referred to as Christ and the woman as the bride of Christ, which is the Church. Each one has a *divine element* within him. It is expedient that we respect and honor the Spirit of God in us.

Yes! The sexual life can affect the spiritual life but the reverse is also true. Sex is predominantly a spiritual thing and the breakthrough for sex problems often begins with prayer. Sex is one hundred percent commitment. It involves every bit of the person's character.

If you want to have a healthy sexual relationship, you cannot just think of sex in terms of biology (the body). Think in terms of psychology because of the involvement of the emotions. Think in terms of philosophy because of the involvement of the mind and also think in terms of the Bible, since the spirit and soul of man is involved. Sex causes two people to commune with one another on the deepest levels of their being and commune with God at the same time. You cannot and must not involve the Spirit of God dwelling in you in sexual immorality.

*"Know ye not that you are the temple of God and **the Spirit of God** dwells in you?"*

189

Consider these scriptures, all these denote sexual intimacy.

"The two shall be one Flesh,"
"Your desire shall be for your husband,"
"Adam knew his wife,"
"Increase and multiply and fill the earth."

Popular sex manuals and the media have deceived the world to accept that sexual fulfillment is simply a matter of biology and emotions. The circular society and even the Church have compromised issues about sex. Little has been achieved in navigating the difference between one's spiritual sex life and emotions. But it is seriously a matter of the spirit and the soul as well.

If you are *not* at peace in your mind and you are not in good spiritual standing with God who created you to be a sexual creature, you cannot expect harmony and fulfillment in your sex life.

Besides, your spiritual growth can be affected by sex either positively or negatively. Beloved are you battling with a sexual problem that seems to have no solution? You cannot control your soul and spirit with your carnal mind and flesh without the power of the Holy Spirit. Take heart, Jesus is still in the business of working miracles. He has full control over every element of your being. He can free you from the fear and the bondage of sex. He is more able and can help you control that fear. Jesus can take away that lustful desire that engages you in illicit sex. He can make you strong in Him to overcome the temptation from sex drive.

Gal. 5:16-18 "So I say, live by the Spirit, and you will not gratify the desires of the sinful nature. For the sinful nature desires what is contrary to the Spirit, and the Spirit what is contrary to the sinful nature. They are in conflict with each

other, so that you do not do what you want. But if you are
led by the Spirit, you are not under law."

Understand that your sex life is wrapped up with your spiritual life. Do not be deceived by Satan to think that sex is the answer to your problem. A man's satisfaction to egoistical passion of sexual desire or a woman's answer to emotional emptiness and loneliness does not come through yielding to the temptation of *the spirit of lust*. Satan tricks people especially the youth and the unmarried to think that real joy; happiness and satisfaction can be found in lust, carnality and perversion.

It is all *lies* and these are deviations from the proper sex life God intended for us to have and enjoy. These lies have nothing to offer but unsatisfied desires, broken hearts, emotional emptiness and slavery to sin.

Precious one, you should refuse to be entangled in Satan's *"sex games and tricks"*. Listen and obey God's command about sex, pray for the power of the Holy Spirit to mold and fill you to be able to stand and wait for God's timing and you will be assured of a happy and enjoyable sex life, purposed by God without any sorrow or heart break attached.

The blessings of God makes rich and adds no sorrow.

The *gift of sex* is one of the numerous blessings of God and must be without sorrow.

CHAPTER TEN

DESTROYING SATAN'S STRONGHOLD ON YOUR MIND AND EMOTIONS

Emotional *guilt* is the *key* to your *defeat*. Let the mind of Christ be in you, which is the fruit of the Holy Spirit.

Let the *righteousness* of Christ fill your mind since that is the *key* to your *victory*.

Jesus was made sin for our sinfulness so that we might be made righteous with His righteousness.

The battlefield of Satan and all evils is the human mind. You must take control over your mind and submit your thoughts to Jesus' thoughts, letting your hearts be filled with joy.

Pray that God, the merciful and loving father cleanse your mind and thoughts from all emotional guilt and plaguing memories.

Prov. 28:13; "he who conceals his sins does not prosper but whoever confesses and renounces them find mercy."

James 5:16; "confess your faults one to another, and pray for one another, that ye may be healed."

Phil 3:14 "I press on toward the goal to win the prize for which God has called me heavenward in Christ Jesus."

Paul stated, forget the past and press on for a better future.

Prayer keys for the Mind

II Cor. 10:5 "we demolish argument and every presentation that sets itself up against the knowledge of God and we take captive every thought to make it obedient to Christ."

Ps. 139:23; "search me oh God and know my heart test me and know my anxious thoughts. See if there is any offensive way in me and lead me in the way everlasting."

Isa. 26:3; "you will keep in perfect and constant peace him whose mind is steadfast, because he trusts in you."

II Tim. 1:7; "for God has not given us the spirit of timidity (fear) but of love, peace and well balanced [sound] mind and discipline and self-control."

Rom. 12:2; "be not conformed to this world but be ye transformed in the renewal of your mind. So that you may prove what is good and acceptable and perfect will of God."

Prayer keys for the Heart

*Ps. 51:10 "create in me a clean heart O God and
renew a right spirit within me."*

*Ps. 19:14; "let the words of my mouth and the meditations
of my heart be acceptable in your sight. O Lord my rock
and my redeemer."*

*Ezek. 11:19; "Then I will give them one heart, and I will
put a new spirit within them, and take the stony heart out of
their flesh, and give them a heart of flesh."*

Prayer keys for the Tongue

*James 1:19 "My dear brothers take note of this: everyone
should be quick to listen and slow to speak and slow to
become angry."*

*James 3:5; "likewise the tongue is a small part of the body,
but it makes great boasts; consider what a great
forest is set on fire by a small spark. The tongue also is a
fire, a world of evil among the parts of the body.
It corrupts the whole body".*

*James 3:8; "But no man can tame the tongue it is a restless
evil full of deadly poison, with the tongue we praise our
Lord and father and with it we curse men who have been
made in God's likeness Out of the same mouth comes praise
and cursing my brothers this should no be so.*

*Prov. 11:13; "a gossip betrays confidence but a
trustworthy man keeps a secret."*

Prov. 16:28 "a perverse man stirs up dissension and a gossip separates close friends."

Gossip hurts, slander kills and sadly both happen among Christians. Negative confession nullifies our prayers. Pronouncement of curses on relations and on ourselves do not glorify God. There is power of life and death on the tongue, so make effort to change your **words** to change your world. You cannot rise above your **words**.

Remember that **miracles** begins from your **mouth**

Your enemy reacts to your **words**

Your enemy will believe whatever you tell him. Speak **faith words** into his ears he will be demoralized. Talk like a **victim** and he will be encouraged to attack you again.

Let your **words** create the current that sweeps you into the heart of God.

Matt 12:27; "for by thy words thou shalt be justified and by thy words thou shalt be condemned."

Prayer keys to Forgiveness

Mark 11:25 "and whenever you stand praying, if you have anything against anyone, forgive him that your father in heaven may also forgive you your trespasses."

Col.3: 13 "bearing with one another and forgiving one another, If anyone has a complaint against another even as Christ forgave you, so you also must do."

Eph. 4:31-32 "let all bitterness, wrath, anger, clamor and evil speaking be put away from you with all malice. And be kind to one another, tender hearted, forgiving one another even as Christ forgave you."

Matt.5: 10 "blessed are those who are persecuted because of righteousness, for theirs is the kingdom of heaven."

Having the spirit of forgiveness is the beginning of enlightenment. It is also peace and happiness.

The unforgiving and resentful spirit is a source of great suffering and sorrow, and he who harbors and encourages it and does not overcome and abandon it, forfeits much blessings.

That individual does not obtain the measure of true enlightenment and joy in life. The hardness of heart is a continual source of suffering. It always takes two to make peace or quarrel, so whatever part that you played in it, do your best as much as it depends on you to live at peace with all men.

Forgiveness is divine, beautiful, sweeter and more effective than revenge. It is indeed healing.

Forgiveness is one of the doorways in the temple of love divine

Prayer keys on Peace

Col.1:20; "and through him (Christ) to reconcile to himself all things, whether things in heaven, by making peace through his blood, shed on the cross."

Col. 3:15; "let the peace of Christ rule in you hearts since as members of one body you were called to peace. And be thankful."

Prov. 14:30; "a heart at peace gives life to the body but envy rots the bones."

John 14:27; "peace I leave with you; my peace I give you. I do not give to you as the world gives. Do not let your heart be troubled and do not be afraid."

Prayer keys to Joy

Neh. 8:10b; "do not grieve, for the joy of the Lord is your strength."

Ps. 51:12; "restore to me the joy of your salvation and grant me a willing spirit to sustain me."

Ps. 43:4; "then I will go to the alter of God, to God, my joy and my delight. I will praise you with the harp. O God my God."

Phil.4: 6 "rejoice in the Lord always and I will say it again: rejoice!"

Prayer keys to Anxiety

1 Peter 5:7; "cast all you're anxiety on him, because he cares for you,"

Phil 4:6; "do not be anxious about anything, but in everything with prayer and supplication with thanksgiving, present your request to God."

THE BATTLE IS IN THE MIND

Eph 6:12; "for we wrestle not against flesh and blood..."

Brothers and sisters we are engaged in warfare where Satan is our *number one* enemy. The battlefield is our mind, and that is where strongholds are set up by the devil. A stronghold is a situation in which we are held in bondage owing to certain ways we think. The combat for which we are to be prepared is not against ordinary human enemies, barely against men compounded of flesh and blood, but against the several ranks of devils that have a government, which they exercise, in the world.

We cannot physically see and fight back the devil or the evil forces known as principalities and powers. This means we are in a spiritual warfare with spiritual enemies.
This makes our battle a serious and dangerous one. So our weapons must surely be a spiritual one.

2 Cor. 10:4-5; "for our weapons are not carnal but mighty through God to the pulling down of strongholds casting down imaginations and every high thing that exalts itself against the knowledge of God and bringing into captivity every thought (state of Mind) to the obedience of Christ."

The amplified translation of this verse of the Bible say; that we are to take these weapons and refute arguments.

That is, to refuse any **negative thought**.

What opposition is made against the gospel by the powers of sin and Satan in the hearts and **minds** of men? — Ignorance, prejudices, beloved lusts are Satan's strongholds in the soul [**mind** will and emotions] of some:

Vain **Imaginations,** carnal reasoning, and **high thoughts** or proud conceits exalt themselves against the knowledge of God.

That is by these ways the devil endeavors to keep men from faith and obedience to the gospel, and secures his possession of the hearts and **minds** of men as his own house or property. The strongholds are pulled down by the grace and power of God accompanying it as the principal efficient cause. Check this:

Rom 12:12 "do not be conformed to this world but be ye transformed (changed) by the renewal of your mind that you may prove what is good and acceptable and perfect will of God."

The good, acceptable and perfect will of God is in obeying His word, following His guidance and being directed by the Holy Spirit. Read *Eph 6:10-18* on the plan of God to fight this warfare. Let the mind of Christ be in you.

God has given us the Bible literally to understand and have His mind. He revealed His mind through His word (Christ). Once we posses His mind, then we are holding His thoughts and the purpose of His heart. That is why you have to make good and positive confessions.

Change your *words* in order to change your *world*.

Understand that the matters of the mind, heart and emotions are very delicate and sensitive. You must take full control of your mind in a total transformational attitude.

The word "heart" is from the Greek word *"Kardia"* which means *"the compartment for your inner self or the seat of your human spirit."*

Be at peace and joyful in your heart and your emotions will also be sound and serene. Heal yourself, let go of all the hurts and receive the peace and the love of God, which will never fail.

Surrender and submit your heart, mind and emotions totally under the power of God. Allow Him to take full control over your life (spirit, soul and body). Remember Satan fights our minds or thoughts and when he succeeds in capturing our mind with evil thoughts, he then conquers our whole being.

Submit yourselves then under the power of God, resist the devil and he will flee away from you. Let God's word and the Holy Spirit radically transform your way of thinking. Renew your mind to know, understand and do the will of God. Pray to Lord Jesus, study, meditate on His word and seek to follow His example.

Be careful of your thoughts because it is capable of ruining your words, actions, habits, character and destiny eventually.

Surrender your heart, mind and emotions unto the Lord.

CHAPTER ELEVEN

Creation Therapy:
Knowing Yourself and Others

As a temperament counselor and an International Representative of Sarasota Academy of Christian Counseling. I cannot close the chapter on this book without making mention of temperaments, which plays a very important role in our behavior, attitudes. It is also a determining factor in many areas of our lives.

"In the beginning God created...." Gen. 1:1

"For you created my inmost being; you knit me together in my mother's womb. I will praise you because I am fearfully and wonderfully made; your works are wonderful, I know that fully well." Psalm 139:14

Creation Therapy is based on the theory of temperament (understanding of the inner man) and uses this knowledge to help us understand ourselves.

Therefore, it allows us to be the best that God has created us to be by meeting the needs of our temperament equally and scripturally.

Although this therapeutic method is a fairly new concept (developed in 1983), it has been extremely successful.

We are fearfully and wonderfully made by our God who created the heavens and the earth. We are very special and unique.

Until now, most of the training in human behavior that has been available to the Christian community has been secular and developed by teachers and writers who clearly believe in evolution.

Understanding who God created you to be will help you to live a victorious Christian life. You will understand your weaknesses and learn how to surrender them to the Lord and, with His help, learn how to develop your strengths.

Paul's question was not *HOW* am I behaving? It was *WHY* am I behaving this way? This information will help you to understand why people do the things they do.

In Hosea 4:6a the Bible states:

"My people are destroyed for lack of knowledge...."

Having this new knowledge will not only draw you closer to the Lord Jesus Christ, it will help you in your relationship with others, e.g. friends, co-workers and family members.
(By Drs. Richard Gene and Phyllis Jean Arno, are the authors of Creation Therapy and the Founders of The Sarasota Academy of Christian Counseling in Sarasota, Florida.)

What is Temperament?

Temperament, in simple terms, is the inborn (not genetic. i.e., brown hair, blue eyes, etc.) but the part of man that determines how he reacts to people, places and things. In short, it is how people interact with their environments and the world around them.

Temperament pinpoints our perception of ourselves and the people who love us. It is also the determining factor in how well we handle the stresses and pressures of life.

Temperament can best be defined as spiritual genetics or God's imprint upon each of us. Three are involved in the conception of a child, the mother, the father, and the Creator.

Temperament is a determining factor in:

a. Finding a career that is most comfortable for us.
b. Finding hobbies that will bring us the most satisfaction and enjoyment.
c. How we can make decisions and take on responsibilities.
d. How dependant or independent we are.
e. Our spiritual development.

Happiness in marriage is greatly dependant on how well each spouse understands his or her partner's temperament and how willing he or she is to meet a partner's temperament needs.

The Building Blocks:

We developed a simple, unique way to break down the complex subject of the "inner man." You may find it helpful for your own understanding and helpful in your attempts to share with others, it is called
"The Building blocks"
*   Self- Selected "Personality" (mask)

- Man/ Environment- Affected "Character" (learned behavior)
- God - Created "Temperament" (inborn)

The first building block for understanding human behavior is **God- created**. This is called our **temperament**. When we are conceived our unique temperament is placed within us by the order of God.

The second building block for understanding human behavior is that we are **man/ environment- affected**- This is called our **"Character."[Learned behavior]**

At birth, we begin to interact with our environment and our environment interacts with us. The environment is everything we see, hear, smell, feel and learn. These perceptions are forever locked into our brain and these things slightly mold and alter our temperament, forming character, (i.e. temperament × environment = character)

The third building block of understanding human behavior is that we are *self- selected*. This is called our **personality**. This may, or may not be part of our temperament or character. This is the way we perceive how we must behave to survive in the world in which we live. There is one major problem with personality. It is a mask we wear for the world and, as with any mask; it cannot be worn for very long.

Eventually, the person must revert back to temperament and character. This explains why a person may act one way at home and a different way in the world.

Three specific areas of Temperament: Inclusion, Control, and Affection:

Inclusion is the need to establish and maintain a satisfactory relationship with people in the area of surface relationships, association, and socialization and intellectual energies.

Control is the need to establish and maintain a satisfactory relationship with people in respect to control and power.

Affection is the need to establish and maintain a satisfactory relationship with others in regard to love and affection.

The Five different Temperaments are:

Melancholy, Choleric, Supine, Phlegmatic and Sanguine.

Melancholy: Rebels, artistic, creative, loners, thinkers, perfectionist, independent and task-oriented.

Choleric: Leaders, task-oriented, organizers, and people- motivators, fast-paced and confident.

Supine: Followers, great capability to serve, gentle spirited, relationship oriented.

Phlegmatic: Negotiators, slow-paced, peacemakers, stubborn, task-oriented, easy-going, low energy.

Sanguine: Friendly, outgoing, inspiring to others, hot tempered, enthusiastic, optimistic, and talkative.

I hope this will serve as useful information to you, to enhance the lives and the quality of the relationship of you and your friends and families.

If you do not know what your temperament is you need to contact me so I can generate a profile for you and detailed information on your temperament analysis or your church counseling center.

Which is your temperament? Melancholy, Choleric, Phlegmatic, Sanguine or Supine? Generate a profile

---

CONCLUSION

We give thanks to God Almighty for His grace, wisdom and knowledge, which He bestowed upon us in this revelational knowledge about women. In Genesis, the woman, Eve, became dissatisfied with all that had been placed in her possession, she disobeyed God, misused her privileges and rights. She made an evil and ambitious choice thereby abusing her position and rights. She lost all she had for an eternal judgment and damnation.

God in His mercies and kindness gave the woman (Eve) a promise of restoration through her Seed. In the fullness of time, by another woman (Mary), God gave mankind an eternal blessing, the gift of His only begotten Son.

In Him and through Him we have our redemption and sanctification by *His precious blood.*

Women must be god-fearing in order to be a blessing to affect their families and the world at large in very positive ways.

What a wonderful, loving mother and wife every woman wishes to be, just as much, all men would wish to have. Women need to be empowered to be effective and make the difference in society. Women empowerment starts right from birth. In empowering women, they must be taught to be prayerful, be knowledgeable about who they are in the Lord, identify their potentials, and work out their vision to fruition.

Marital issues are very complex and challenging, and therefore needs much caution and proper preparation. The young woman must be fulfilled as a genuinely submissive wife who remains in her *"pure original state"* until her wedding day. As a woman, when you remain obedient to God and those in authority, you will be blessed to be virtuous, more precious and valuable than gold.

Disobedience is the gateway to all sins. All young unmarried women should make every effort to keep their virginity (chastity), just like the Blessed Virgin Mary and queen Esther, in order to be highly favored, with glory and honor. Young girls should be virtuous in order to become virtuous women. Preserve yourselves as a living sacrifice.

Rom. 12:1 "I beseech thee brethren therefore by the mercies of God, that ye present your bodies a living sacrifice, holy acceptable unto God, which is your reasonable service".

To the older women maintain your salvation and sanctification. The writer of *Proverbs 31:10-31* dared to present the picture of a woman as glorious, vibrant, competent and intelligent creation of God. A virtuous woman or a woman of noble character wears many faces; and fills many roles that can change with the season of her life. In essence she draws her strength to lay down her life for God, her family and the nation at large.

I pray the favor, blessing and honor of God on all women. Just as Lemuel's [Solomon] mother gave godly advice to her son so also elderly women and mothers must give good advice to their sons and daughters. Young men must be discrete and faithful, avail themselves to be used of God.

They should avoid unhealthy relationships, flee their youthful lust and control their *'sex drive' as young men of integrity.* Fathers be more responsible and caring, do not *provoke your children.*

Finally if we claim to love Christ we must obey His Commandments:

> *John 14:23; Jesus replied "if anyone loves me he will obey my teachings."*

> *1 Sam. 15:22; "to obey is better than sacrifice."*

Remember it does not matter the circumstance around you, what shame, failure, guilt or rejection you may be going through. It doesn't matter if those who once confessed to be lovers of your soul are now your enemies. Judas did it to Jesus by betraying Him with a kiss.

Beware! Not all kisses are kisses of love.

Some are kisses of betrayal.

Some are kisses of deceit.

Some are hatred and some rejection.

Which of these have you had?

What do you think was the motive or intent behind the kiss? Forget forgive and take it to the Lord in prayer.

What matters is, God is your shield, glory and your honor. Jesus Christ your permanent husband and the great redeemer is the one who has saved you and He is always available for you. He is your strength and has taken away your shame and sins, just as He has done for me.

You must refuse to be trodden upon, know that life indeed is a process and there is a price to pay for every great achievement. Accept your challenges with love and in good faith as a price you are paying for a great and precious future.

APOSTOLIC BLESSINGS

Dear reader, may you be the woman God desires you to be. May the Lord be your shield, your glory, honor and the lifter-up of your head, according to:

> *Psalm 3:3 "for thou, O Lord, art a shield for me; my glory and the lifter up of mine head."*

May the Lord remain the lifter up of your head till you achieve the best of God for your life and walk in your high places.

May Lord bless and keep you; the Lord the make His faces shine upon you and be gracious to you. The Lord lift up His countenance upon you and give you peace.

May God Richly Bless You!

In case you are not saved pray this prayer from your heart sincerely today!

Dear Lord Jesus I want to know you personally.

Thank you for dying on the cross for my sins. I repent of all my sins.

I open the door of my life and receive you as my Lord and Savior. Thank you for forgiving me all of my sins, and giving me eternal life. Take full control of my life. Make me the kind of person you want me to be in Jesus name. Amen!

If you said this prayer in faith and in sincerity of heart, then precious one, you are born again.

I encourage you to find a good Bible believing Church to join so you can grow in your walk with the LORD.

ENDORSEMENTS

PROFILE OF DR. LUTTERODT

I Witnessed her being born again and growing through the word, to be a spirit filled woman.

Through her development and maturity in the Lord, she continued to various Bible schools where she was prepared to enter into ministry with a special assignment into Woman Ministry. Life's challenges and experiences have given her a heart for women and to reach out to women in order to affect their lives in a more positive way.

The '*price*' she had to pay to be where she is now, and to be able to come out with '*The Virtuous Woman*,' qualifies her into ministering to women aspiring to lead a more

honorable and valued life. She has indeed been of great blessing and impact to women in the cities, through her TV and Radio programs, where she had ministered. She has ministered especially in my Church, Calvary Life

International Church. I am most grateful to God almighty for her life.

By Rev. Divine Adjei, President and founder,
Calvary Life International Church,
Kumasi Ghana.

Dr. Kate Lutterodt was a student of the School of the Word, where she finished with a diploma in Ministerial Training. She proceeded to train at World Mission Bible Institute, where she has another diploma in Integrated Mission Theology and Associate of Art Theology. On the

6th of April 2002, having been examined as qualified to be a minister of the gospel; she was ordained and commissioned into the ministry of the gospel of Jesus Christ.

This woman demonstrated her calling through the preaching of the undiluted truth of the gospel during the Minister's club seminar, church programs and other gospel outreach. She had taught at different women's seminar and conferences on the subject of the '*virtuous woman.*'

Her expositions of the Bible on the basic principles of the Virtuous Woman have really given her popularity in the gospel circle in the region. She was a major T.V. speaker, as the producer and presenter of '***The Virtuous Woman***'. She is a member and a close associate of the Prayer of Faith Ministry.

I hereby recommend Dr Kate Lutterodt for the gospel outfit anywhere in the world, based on her outstanding success in ministry and especially on this exceptional write up: '*The Virtuous Woman*'.

Rev. Dr. Edward Ade (Rector, World Mission Bible Institute, General Overseer, Prayer of Faith Ministries International) Kumasi Ghana.

The book '*The Virtuous Woman*' has become one of the best tools for development for the youths who desire to become the woman of *Proverbs 31.* The timing of this book could not have been better at a time when society is losing sight of the importance of Christian values and character. Dr. Kate Lutterodt has successfully put her experience and knowledge of the word to bring enlightenment and attention to critical issues pertaining to women and to the men in their lives. I applaud Dr. Kate Lutterodt for a job well done!

Dr. Lucianna Davies, C.L.G.
Maryland, U.S.A

We are living in perilous days, days where *HIV/AIDS* is sweeping through the world like a flood. Days when the choice to engage in sex has become a choice between life and death especially in Africa.

This book 'The *Virtuous Woman' provides* timely and biblically sound guidance to our young ladies as they make life-changing decisions. It will be a great blessing to those who read it and obey the godly- instructions therein.

Dr. Ebby Anyamba
Missions Director, C.L.G.
Maryland U.S.A.

Thank you Dr. Kate Lutterodt for writing such a stimulating, eye opening and spiritually challenging book. The credibility of the '*Virtuous Woman*'' is packed with learnable concepts that do more than just to educate it really stimulates and enlightens.

Rev. Dr. & Mrs. Chinedum Brown C.L.G
Pastor I/C Richmond Virginia, U.S.A.

Dr. Lutterodt is a woman who honors the Lord. God has used her mightily in her country Ghana and has sent her to the USA to be a blessing.

Her book, '*The Virtuous Woman*' presents a step-by-step plan on how women can live in the freedom that Jesus Christ died to provide. This book is filled with scriptures, which are the keys to unlock the glorious moral graces, which are the foundation for the husband and wife relationship.

I heartily endorse this book and pray that it will have wide circulation in the USA and around the world.

Dr. William M. Comfort D.Phil, N.D., F.I.B A
President/founder Chesapeake Bible College &
Seminary
Ridgley MD.U.S.A.

For questions and speaking engagements:

CONTACT INFORMATION

DR. KATE LOVE LUTTERODT;
VIRTUOUS WOMAN COUNSELLING & OUTREACH
MINISTRY.
(Los Angeles California.)
E-mail: virtuouswomankl@yahoo.com
Web site: www.thevwcom.com.
Tel: 213-265-5900
Fax: 213 -480 -0883.

Look out for the next books, coming out:

"THE MAN OF INTEGRITY"

We cannot talk of women being virtuous without a word to men. For a woman to be virtuous and remain virtuous for the rest of her life, she needs a faithful man, indeed a man of integrity.

Prov. 20:6b; "A faithful man who can find."

To a woman, the man is the most complex of all God's creatures. He has high hopes and expectations for himself. He experiences emotions that are difficult to handle if he fails to attain his dream.

At times, he is afraid of rejection, being compared to another man, he may struggle with the ability to satisfy his wife.

He may feel inadequate, insecure, frustrated and helpless as he faces the challenges of life.

During these times of vulnerability, a man desperately needs an understanding helper.

Gen 2:18 say "And the Lord God said, it is not good that the man should be alone, I will make him a help mate who is comparable to him."

Just as the man needs the virtuous woman to help him fulfill his God given assignment, so does the woman need a faithful man, a man of integrity, that entire man that God has created for her. This task is not only to the husband, but men in general.

You must all strive to be men of integrity to the women in your lives whether you are a father, husband, brother or an uncle,

Prov. 20:6 says "most men will proclaim every one his own goodness: but a faithful man who can find?"

A faithful, sincere and a kind man who can find?

It is not easy to find a virtuous woman just as to finding a man who really has affection to do well.

Men who have charity, generosity, hospitality, piety and a kind heart. *Proverbs 19:22* state what is desired in man is his *kindness.*

Loving-kindness is what we desire in others and God desires it in us as well.

Such kindness or mercy is an evidence of wisdom and should be demonstrated in godly living. Any one who practices unfailing love draws one to himself.

Wives and children should know and see kindness in their husbands and fathers.

NUGGETS FOR THE MAN OF INTEGRITY

He communicates well with his wife and dwells with her according to knowledge: Not according to lust as brutes.

Not according to passion as devils, but according to knowledge. As wise and sober, as men who know the word of God and their god -given duties.

The man of integrity gives honor to his wife and gives due respect to her in maturity.

He is not despotic or authoritative but rather protects her personality and supporting her credit.

He delights in her conversation, affording her best of maintenance.

Placing due trust and confidence in her.

Job was a model of a man of integrity, the character study for this book.

Job 1:1*; "Job was a man who was blameless and upright and one who feared God and eschewed evil".*

Job was a wealthy man full of love for God. God tested his love for Him by allowing Satan to tempt him.

Job went through a lot of hardship but stood firm, steadfastly in faith and did not curse God in his trials.

Job was a man of faith, patience and endurance, known as a generous and caring person.

Job kept himself from secret sins, his goodness kept him away from it. Job suffered pain in sickness in the body under affliction, and sustained it through.

Men likewise in the same manner must be able to maintain their love and allegiance to God during great trials in life. They should be careful to preserve their bodies in holiness and to possess their vessels in sanctification, honor and purity from the lust of uncleanness.

Job said, "I have made a covenant with my eyes not to look upon a virgin."

By this he meant that the grace of God has kept him from the very first step toward sin. What do you allow your eyes to see? Men need the fear and Spirit of God to restrain them from such sins in order to be men of integrity. To read more pray and look out towards the soon coming *"of **The** of **Man Integrity**".*

WHAT DOES THE BIBLES SAY ABOUT WOMEN MINISTERS? *[as God's Servants]*

"Ten reasons why the Bible teaches Women in ministry, [to be in the service of God]

There have been arguments, controversies, and church traditions not to mention the general perceptions on the question of if women should be in Ministry? My extensive research on this topic helped me to dig into these and many more truths:

I. Women played important role in the Team Ministry.
2. God used female ministers in the Old Testament.
3. The first person to have personal encounter with Jesus was the Blessed Virgin Mary[*Mother of the promised of Seed*]
4. The Pentecost experience changed the inferiority of the Women.
5. Households became House Churches for women-leaders and teachers.
6. Women were the financial backbone of the Gospel and Jesus' traveling ministry.
7. Women played most prominent role at the resurrection.
8. There were female counterparts for the different ministries.
9. Jesus elevated women into Ministries.
10. Clarification of the one-sided erroneous interpretation.

Some of the arguments and controversies of gender barrier, in the Gospel Ministry has been fully ascertained. That is women as well as men are called and have God's authority and authentication to be in ministry. Women like Miriam, Phoebe, Deborah, Mary Magdalene and many more have left behind a great legacy and challenge for women to emulate.

Women at the resurrection contributed to pull down the walls of gender barrier.

Thank God for the Bible Patriarchs who left us such vital information and 'eye opener', the Holy Spirit who continues to prepare, refresh, anoint and empower all, both men and women in ministry.

*Eph 4:11-13 "And He gave some, **Apostles;** and some **Prophets;** and some **Evangelist;** and some **Pastors and Teachers.** For the perfecting of the saints, for the **work** of the **ministry,** for the edifying of the body of Christ; till we **all** come in the **unity** of the faith, and the knowledge of the Son of God, unto the measure of the stature of the fullness of **Christ."***

This is the **5-fold ministry** they are all from the same God to **all** who have been called into ministry. Thus they carry the same level of anointing and mantel, none is greater than the other.

It is my prayer and desire that all women be challenged, whether married or not married. No color, ethnicity or gender barrier should discourage women from taking their place in ministry in any of the ministries mentioned above.

However it is necessary to emphasize here the importance of humility; submissiveness and wisdom that women need to exhibit in pursuing their ministry goals. This is an excerpt from my thesis on the course,

"What does the Bible say about Women Ministers?"

PT220.Women in Ministry pray and watch out! for this book

POETRY

MEANINGS OF WOMAN

Who knows me? Who can tell my name?
My name is **WOMAN**.
Don't just know my name but know what I mean as well.
I begin with *"W"*, which stands for **WORSHIP**.
Who can worship more than me? Let any man protest,
I will go and call my Auntie Mary Magdalene, and she will tell you it was she who used her hair to wipe the perfume off Jesus' feet. Now tell me where could one's body be if the hair were right at the feet of someone?
Is it not on the floor?
As Miriam I worshipped God after He had taken us through the Red sea. I am proud to be a woman just because ''W'' helps me to fulfill the purpose of God creating human beings.
In the Church I set the wheel of worship going. My scream alone causes people to climb to the heavenly throne to say to God; the moon and stars shows your glory.
My next letter is *"O"* and it means **OFFERING**,
Who can offer and compete with me in terms of offering?
As Hannah, I offered Samuel to the service of God.
As a widow, I offered my last morsel of bread to Elijah, the prophet. As Ruth, I offered my country to follow Naomi, a woman of God.

As Martha, I offered my food to serve Jesus and His numerous followers.

As Mary Magdalene, I offered my precious perfume to prepare Jesus for burial. As the widow I offered my last penny and Jesus recommended me. I tell you, with me in the church, she (church) is blessed.

The next letter in my name is *"M"* and it means *MEDIUM*. I am the medium through which important personalities emerge. When the Savior's 'court crier' (forerunner) John the Baptist was coming, it was I Elizabeth who was used.

I, Mary was the right medium to be used when God had to be transformed into man. Am I not great?

Right in the church it is I, who give most of the prophecies.

Also because of my special voice, it is I who always gives vote of thanks at occasions. As a medium, I will always make myself available for the glory of God.

My last but one letter is *"A"* for *ASSISSTANCE,* because of this God needed assistance before creating me.

As the last born of God, I am pampered. My mission on earth therefore is to assist man to perform his duties.

How could Abraham become friend of God without my assistance?

As a woman, Sarah, my food alone could make the angels going to destroy Sodom and Gomorah reveal the secret to Abraham. I killed Barak without the assistance of any man. As Deborah, I used my wisdom to judge Israel. As Abigail, my husband did not die in the hands of David just because of my assistance.

My last letter is *"N"* and it stands for *"NEWS"*

Who was the first to hear the news of Christ's birth? It was I Mary; angel Gabriel appeared to and gave the good news. Again it was I who first reported the resurrection of Jesus.

In Samaria, I, the woman at the well was the first evangelist who sent the news.

All over the world I *the woman* possess news, process news and propagate news. If you want news just contact, a woman, and as a Christian woman, I will give you the good news from God.

Yes, this is me you've known now, call me **WOMAN**.

But remember *I* stand for **WORSHIP, OFFERING, MEDIUM, ASSISSTANCE AND NEWS.**

(Written by: Grace Adu, U.C. C, Ghana)

ACRONYMS OF PRECIOUS

P - *II Cor 11:2 "might present you as **pure** virgin "*
R – *1 Peter 2:17 "show proper **r**espect to everyone."*
E – *Rom. 15:4 through **en**durance and encouragement…"*
C – *II Cor. 16: 9 "those whose hearts are fully **committed**'*
I – *1 Tim. 2:1 "intercession and thanksgiving be made…"*
O - **Isaiah 1:19: "if ye are** obedient **ye shall eat the good of the land."**
U – *Eph. 1:18 "understanding the hope to which He has called us."*
S – *I Cor. 6:11 "…. but ye were washed, ye were sanctified."*

I Thessalonians 5:21-23

"Test everything. Hold on to the good. Avoid every kind of evil. May God Himself, the God of peace, sanctify you through and through. May your whole spirit, soul and body be kept blameless at the coming of our Lord Jesus Christ. The one who calls you is faithful and He will do it."

231

REFLECTIONS /
NOTES ON THE CHAPTERS:

Testimony; Attempted abortion
The 'unaborted baby'
Aborted or thinking of aborting your blessing?
Is abortion a woman's right or sin?

Chapter one
The Mystery of Womanhood.
The first fruit of God
The pure original state
Virginity/sealed state
Hymen
Rape/Sexual sin

Chapter two
Creation / significance of woman
Garden of Eden / paradise
Rib taken from Adam to form Eve
First second third significance
Why woman was created
Purpose / plan of God
Help –mate, companion
Co- habitation
So shall a man leave and cleave
Man [Adam] stands for Christ
Woman [Eve] stands for The Church of Christ

Chapter three
Disobedience & disrespect typical characters of women
Saw the fruit good for food; lust of the eye
Appealing to appetite; lust of the flesh
Enticing ambition; pride of life
Character Study
Disobeyed God /disrespected her husband of life
Weaknesses /evil aspects of women
Crowning qualities of women
Biblical rights of women

Chapter four
The fall of our first parents
Eve tempted/defeated/transgression
Sentence passed on Eve, Adam & Satan
First, second & third aspect of the fall
The ultimate consequences of sin
State of sorrow subjection
Expulsion from the Garden of Eden
God's care after sin

Chapter five
Steps to be a Virtuous Woman
Repentance, regeneration,
Sanctification, justification &adoption
Expository of Proverbs 31; 10-28
Other practical qualities of a Virtuous Woman
Tips for the young virtuous lady

Chapter six
The Two shall be one
Dating/Courtship in the Christian perspective
Are you single whole &complete?
Marriage the Bible way
Family order/divorce

Chapter Seven
Why women ministry in the church
The call or challenge of Titus 2:3-5
Wonderful promises in Prov. chapter 3 awaiting the young
person who chooses God's way; an incomparable prize
Spiritual Empowerment
Rights and responsibilities of mothers and elderly women

Chapter eight
The woman that God uses
A Vessel of honor sanctified for the Master's use.
Hindrances to Holiness
The three Veils; flesh mind heart
Access to Holy of Holies
Revelation of spiritual nakedness
Ways that God uses us; Spiritual/motivational gifts
Identify your gift to the service of God

Chapter nine
Soul-Ties; Matters of the heart, mind &emotion
Godly/ungodly soul-ties
Dangers of ungodly soul-ties the strongest human
covenant
Sexuality & spirituality

Chapter ten
Destroying Satan's strong hold on our minds and
Emotions
Prayer keys for the Tongue
Prayer keys on Forgiveness, Peace, Joy &, Anxiety
The battle is in the mind

Chapter eleven
Creation Therapy
Temperament defined

The five different temperaments
Generate a profile

ABOUT THE AUTHOR

D r. Kate Love Lutterodt, is a vessel anointed, appointed and set apart by God for His use.

Dr. Kate Love Lutterodt was called into ministry in 1997/98.

She has ministered in many charismatic churches in Ghana and has been a blessing in the establishment of Women fellowship groups.

Dr. Lutterodt has a strong passion for the well being of the family especially young and old women. Her heart's desire is to see young women married properly according to principles set out in God's word.

She also wants to see women rise and shine as they take their place of prominence in the things of God to become what God has called them to be in the church and society at large. Based on her calling, she enrolled at the School of the Word (Part of 'House of Faith Ministries') where she completed with a diploma in Ministerial Training.

Dr. Lutterodt then proceeded to World Missions Bible Institute. Upon completion, she received another diploma in Integrated Missions Theology and Associate of Art Theology.

She had the privilege to minister to women on a local TV station (Crystal TV) and FM stations all in Kumasi, Ghana including churches and women programs with her message about the *'Virtuous Woman' [Prov. 31:10]*

On arriving in the U.S.A., her passion for women enabled her to pursue women ministry education in leadership with a training course through the National Women's Ministry Department of Assemblies of God and was certified as a National Women's Leader.

In the year 2005, Dr. Lutterodt continued and completed her education at Chesapeake Bible School & Seminary in Baltimore Maryland with certificate of Achievement in 'Women in Ministry' (PT220).

In the same year 2005 she received Bachelors degree in Christian Ministry and Masters in Pastoral Counseling through an accelerated programme. With great zeal and of course all by His grace.

Dr. Kate Lutterodt finally graduated with a Doctorate in Clinical Pastoral Counseling in 2006, and was the distinguished honored graduate of 2006. She majored in Creation Therapy, which is based the on theory of Temperament; understanding of the inner man of a person, by generating a profile with the A.P.S. (Arno Profile System), to show them how to meet their needs in ways pleasing to God.

This is through the [NCCA] National Christian Counselors Association in Florida USA.

She is a multi-gifted woman of God: An author and writer, a teacher, evangelist and an Advanced Certified Licensed Clinical Pastoral Counselor.

She is also a Certified Temperament Counselor and a Professional Clinical Member of [NCCA]. Dr. Lutterodt is an International Representative of Sarasota Academy of Christian Counseling in Florida.

She is also a Licensed Advanced Certified International Chaplain.

She is part of the Evangelist/Missionary fellowship, one of the Sunday-School staff and one of the professors of the Bible College at West Angeles Church of God in Christ, Los Angeles, California.

Dr. Lutterodt is the president and founder of *The Virtuous Woman Counseling & Outreach Ministry.*

This is a ministry greatly concerned with the [P.E.M.S]

Physical, **E**motional, **M**ental and **S**piritual needs and well being of the family especially women, this is indeed our heartbeat.

This is the ministry where the unsaved, divorced, hurting, broken-hearted, drugs and alcohol dependants find hope in God.

Also the depressed and the destitute can find love, guidance, encouragement and liberty.

They can be delivered from any form of bondage and oppression with the help of God.

NOTES

NOTES

NOTES

NOTES

NOTES

NOTES

<u>NOTES</u>

The Tiny Turtle with the Yellow Specks

JOHANN-CASPAR ISEMER

The Tiny Turtle

with the

Yellow Specks

children's book by
Johann-Caspar Isemer

Learn more about the book at
isemer.com/turtle